THE

STATUTES AND REGULATIONS,

INSTITUTES, LAWS

AND

GRAND CONSTITUTIONS

OF THE

Ancient and Accepted Scottish Rite.

COMPILED, WITH NOTES, FROM AUTHENTIC DOCUMENTS,

FOR THE USE OF THE ORDER.

BY ALBERT PIKE, 33d,

M∴ P∴ SOVEREIGN GRAND COMMANDER OF THE SUPREME COUNCIL FOR THE SOUTHERN JURISDICTION
OF THE UNITED STATES.

1859

The Statutes and Regulations, Institutes, Laws and Grand Constitutions
of the Ancient and Accepted Scottish Rite
by Albert Pike
foreword by Michael R. Poll

Published by Cornerstone Book Publishers
An Imprint of Michael Poll Publishing
Copyright © 2013 by Cornerstone Book Publishers

Cornerstone Book Publishers
New Orleans, LA

Part of the Cornerstone Scottish Rite Education Series

First Cornerstone Edition - 2013

www.cornerstonepublishers.com

ISBN: 1613421168
ISBN-13: 978-1-61342-116-1

MADE IN THE USA

Masonry is engaged in her crusade, - against ignorance, intolerance, fanaticism, superstition, uncharitableness, and error.

~ Albert Pike
Morals and Dogma

Foreword
The Grand Constitutions of 1786
by Michael R. Poll

This important 1859 work provides us with a copy of the Constitutions of 1762 and the Grand Constitutions of 1786. The later is the collection that was accepted as the rule and law of the early Ancient and Accepted Scottish Rite. No student of the Scottish Rite should be ignorant of these documents nor fail to study them. While both of these collections should be understood, this foreword addresses the Grand Constitutions of 1786 as they were the focus of so much scrutiny during the whole of the 1800's. In fact, few Masonic documents have been debated, praised, maligned, studied and misunderstand more than the collection known as the Grand Constitutions of 1786. There are actually two collections with that name, one known as the French version and the other as the Latin version. But what are they, why are they important, and why all the fuss about them?

The Grand Constitutions of 1786 are directly associated with the 33-degree Ancient and Accepted Scottish Rite and are its original rules and regulations. The first Scottish Rite Supreme Council was created in Charleston, South Carolina on May 31, 1801 and used the Grand Constitutions both as authority to exist and laws for governance. The Grand Constitutions of 1786 provided the first Supreme Council with a blueprint, and it gave them guidance in the organization, structure and management of the new system.

In the early days of the Scottish Rite, the Grand Constitutions were perceived to be of great importance to the young Supreme Council, but were of no value to Grand Lodges who often viewed the new system as mere side degrees. For the Scottish Rite, they were not only central to the government of the system, but could also be used as evidence of legitimacy. In fact, the original Charleston Supreme Council (today officially known as "The Supreme Council [Mother Council of the World] of the Inspectors General Knights Commander of the House of the Temple of Solomon of the Thirty-third degree of the Ancient and Accepted Scottish Rite of Freemasonry of the Southern Jurisdiction of the United States of America" – but more commonly known simply as the "Southern

Jurisdiction") did use the Grand Constitutions as evidence of legitimacy in what would become a "Scottish Rite war" spanning most of the 19th century.

John Mitchell was the first Grand Commander of the Charleston Council (i.e., the "Southern Jurisdiction"). Mitchell had been a Deputy Inspector General (25°) of an older Masonic system known as the Order of the Royal Secret, more commonly known as the Rite of Perfection. In 1807, when Joseph Cerneau, another Deputy Inspector General of the Order of the Royal Secret, created bodies in New York that would evolve into a second Supreme Council in the United States, the young Charleston Council used the Grand Constitutions to argue that this second council was unauthorized and irregular. In 1813, Emanuel de la Motta, an Active Member of the Charleston Council, traveled to New York and – with or without the knowledge or approval of the Charleston Council – created a second Supreme Council in New York on August 23, 1813, to usurp the Cerneau creation. This council would become the Northern Masonic Jurisdiction known today as the partner to the Southern Jurisdiction.

Interestingly enough, the Northern Masonic Jurisdiction (NMJ) and the Southern Jurisdiction (SJ) have historically disagreed over which version of the Grand Constitutions of 1786 they accept. The NMJ accepts the French version, and the SJ the Latin version. But why should there be different versions of a document that would seem to be crucial to the Scottish Rite? What and where is the original?

The Grand Constitutions of 1786 contain 18 Articles, or laws, and it was reported to be approved and signed in Berlin by Frederic the Great on May 1, 1786. Unfortunately, the original document is not known to exist. When the Charleston Council demanded the Cerneau Council produce documentation showing it was authorized to exist, the Cerneau Council produced nothing. The Charleston Council labeled Cerneau unauthorized and irregular. When the Cerneau Council demanded that the Charleston Council prove that they were authorized to exist, the Charleston Council pointed to its copy of the Grand Constitutions of 1786. The Cerneau Council dismissed this document as a forgery and accused the rival group of hypocrisy. The Cerneau Council claimed it had the same right and authority to exist as did the Charleston Council, and that the standards of legitimacy should be the same for both.

Another claim made by the Charleston Council was that any additional Supreme Council created in the United States needed its approval, which it did *not* give to Cerneau.

So, who, if anyone, was correct? Is it possible that the Grand Constitutions of 1786 are a forgery and they were never approved by Frederic? Let's have a look at the two versions of the Grand Constitutions of 1786. Of the French version, Albert Pike tells us:

> "If I were satisfied that there never were any other Constitutions than those contained in the French version, I should not hesitate to admit that they were a clumsy forgery, and that there was nothing in the world to prove them authentic."[1]

Those are very strong words! But why would Pike write such a strong denunciation of this French version? Past SJ Sovereign Grand Commander Henry Clausen explains that "Pike's [Latin] version is obviously a truer copy of the original because it supplies omissions and corrections that were apparent in the French version."

"Following are a few examples from Pike's pen showing the disparity between the French and the Latin versions:

"The French Constitutions neither provide for nor describe any Jewel or Cordon of the Degree. The Seal is described as 'a large BLACK Eagle with two heads, the beak of gold, the wings displayed, and holding in its claws a naked sword; upon a ribbon displayed below is written DUES MEUMQUE JUS, and above the Eagle, SUPREME COUNCIL OF THE 33rd DEGREE. [Official Bulletin, Vol. V, No.2, p. 548]

"The French Constitutions provide for one Council of the Degree in each Nation or Kingdom in Europe; for two in the United States of America; for one in the British West Indies; and one in the French West India Islands. But none is provided for Canada; none for the Province of Louisiana, or the Spanish Possessions in North America; and none for South America. [Official Bulletin, Vol. VII, No. 1, p. 486]

"Their Article VI provides that 'the power of the Supreme Council does not interfere in any Degree below the 17th;' and Article VII that only Councils or individuals above the Grand Council of Princes of Jerusalem may bring their appeal to the Supreme Council. This was necessary, in 1801, at Charleston, to prevent hostility on the part of the Grand Lodge of Perfection and Grand Council of Princes of Jerusalem, then and theretofore existing in South Carolina. Why was it necessary in 1786, in Prussia, where no Lodge of Perfection or Council of Princes of Jerusalem existed? [Ibid., p.487]

"The fees for the 33rd Degree and for the Patent of it are expressed to be payable, not in German, but in French coin. [Ibid., p.487]" [2]

Pike's rational and categorical reproof of the French version makes it difficult to understand how one could, with any understanding of Pike's argument and its implications, reasonably defend the French version. Yet, this is the very version that the NMJ accepts. Why? Even more interesting is the fact that Pike himself used the French version to support his position in a Masonic debate. In the 1860s, the Supreme Councils of the NMJ and SJ entered into a debate over territory. Josiah Drummond, the Grand Commander of the NMJ, and Albert Pike, the Grand Commander of the SJ, debated jurisdictional questions over certain states. Drummond wrote to Pike in 1868:

"I hold that under the Constitutions of 1786, the Northern Jurisdiction and the Southern Jurisdiction are, in every respect and for all purposes, as distinct as if they were separate nations: that we, as well as you, derive our rights of jurisdiction from those Constitutions; that those Constitutions create two separate Jurisdictions. On the other hand, I perceive, that you have held that your Supreme Council had jurisdiction throughout North America, and that we get our territory by cession from you; and if by cession, consequently we get only such territory as you choose to cede: and as necessary, that there could have been

no Supreme Council in this Jurisdiction unless you had chosen to cede us territory."[3]

How did Pike answer Drummond? He wrote (arguing the meaning of certain phrases in the French version):

"I do not agree that the Constitutions created the two Jurisdictions. For the United States composed a single Jurisdiction until 1813 or 1815, and might have continued to be as such until today. The provision is restrictive — that there shall not be *more than two* Supreme Councils established in the United States. That is the real meaning of it; not that there shall be two. But the point is of no practical importance, and I pass it.... If Illustrious Brother Drummond were right in holding that the Northern part of the United States did not belong to the Jurisdiction of the Southern Council, prior to 1813 or 1815, but was to vest, whether it willed it or not, in a Northern Council, whenever one should be created there, a consequence which he does not foresee might follow. That hypothesis would make the Northern states to have been unoccupied territory, in which any Inspector General could establish a Supreme Council; and it might thus make legitimate the Cerneau Council, and annihilate that created in 1813 or 1815 by De la Motta. It certainly would destroy the principal ground on which the legitimacy of Cerneau's Council was always impeached; to-wit, that the Council at Charleston had jurisdiction over the whole United States, and that no other Council could be created any where in them, except with its consent." [4]

Pike and Drummond were debating the meaning of Article Five of the French version, which determined the number of Supreme Councils allowed in the US. This debate resulted in Pike producing quite lengthy arguments concerning French and English grammar and the reasons for his position concerning the meaning of Article Five of the French version. Pike even changed a portion of the English translation in his Grand Constitutions to reflect his opinion of the rendition.[5] In his 1868 Allocution, Pike very skillfully debated this

interpretation of Article Five of the French version at length and he did likewise in his Grand Constitutions. But why should Pike bother to painstakingly argue a point concerning a document that he had dismissed as a "clumsy forgery"? Pike should have, for the sake of clearly articulating his true position, debated the Latin version — which he claimed to be legitimate. Why didn't he? Simply put, Pike could not debate this portion of the Latin version. The same portion of Article Five of the Latin version (the version Pike refers to as the "law of the Rite")[6] reads:

> "In each great nation of Europe, and in each Kingdom or Empire, there shall be but one single Supreme Council of this Degree. In all those States and Provinces, as well of the mainland as of the islands, whereof North America is composed, there shall be two Councils, one at as great a distance as may be from the other." [7]

Pike strongly contended that the meaning of Article Five (French version) was that the US was not required to be divided into two jurisdictions, yet that is exactly the meaning of the Latin version, which Pike himself had published in 1859 in this very book that you are reading. Pike used the French version in his debate with Drummond simply because it was more open to interpretation. The "consequence" that Pike claimed would follow if Drummond's interpretation was accepted, is clearly present in the Latin version — Cerneau, it seems, might have had reason, based on the version of the Grand Constitutions accepted by the SJ, to believe that he had rightfully established his Council.

The problem for Drummond was that Pike had skillfully painted him into a corner with his masterful use of Drummond's preferred French version. The territorial debate ended with Drummond yielding to Pike's demands. The view held by Drummond, however, was not only based on his interpretation of Article Five of the French version, but also on the "birth certificate" of the Northern Council itself, which reads in part:

> "And whereas the Grand Constitutions of the 33° specifies particularly, that there shall be two Grand & Supreme Councils of the 33d Degree for the Jurisdiction of the United

States of America, one for the South and the other for the North."[8]

It is obvious why Drummond interpreted Article V of the French version as he did. The NMJ was created on the premise that the constitutions provided for two councils in the United States. Its only contention could have been if Cerneau was not a legitimate Sovereign Grand Inspector General; after all, if he was legitimate, the Cerneau Council was perfectly legal and the NMJ was – by its own stated reason for being created – unauthorized! Pike's opinions concerning the meaning of the original French interpretation were clearly not shared by Emanuel de la Motta, who created the NMJ and was an active Member of the original Charleston Council. It is, likewise, evident why Pike's "threats" might well have been taken seriously. Clearly the only available attack that could reasonably be made on Cerneau, from the NMJ perspective, was to discredit his legitimacy as a SGIG – but great care had to be taken in this course of action as there is no reason to believe Cerneau and John Mitchell obtained the degree in any different manner.[9] To discredit Cerneau's 33rd might also discredit Mitchell's.

It would seem apparent that Pike was unaware of the existence of a handwritten copy of the French version of the Grand Constitutions that had been made by Frederick Dalcho, the first Lt. Grand Commander of the Charleston Council and its second Grand Commander following John Mitchell; the document was not discovered until the 20th century.[10] (This copy now resides in the Kloss Collection in the Grand Lodge Library, The Netherlands, which also includes a manuscript of the Ritual of the Thirty-third Degree.) Pike boldly proclaimed the French version a fraud, and offered very lucid support for his position, while clearly having no idea of the pernicious wording of the "birth certificate" of the NMJ. An additional problem for Pike was that the Latin version was unknown before 1832. To make matters worse, it was none other than a Cerneau Council that made the Latin version available to the world.[11]

Customarily, papers discussing Joseph Cerneau include arguments concerning the Grand Constitutions of 1786. Cerneau is routinely accused of acting in violation of these Constitutions. Nineteenth-century defenders of Cerneau typically argued the lack

of authenticity of the Grand Constitutions, with the apparent belief that if the Grand Constitutions could be discredited then all charges against Cerneau would likewise be dismissed. One claim that was often made was that Frederic the Great had been in very poor heath at the time the Constitutions were said to be approved, and that he was physically unable to have given them consent. Albert Pike went to great lengths to examine the charge that Frederic was not physically able to have executed such a document. Pike meticulously traced the reported events and laid out a detailed report on his position that it was possible for Frederic to have executed the Grand Constitutions. Scottish Rite historian Samuel Baynard of the NMJ writes of Pike's conclusions:

> "Though we admit that our Illustrious Brother did in a masterly manner fully convince us that Frederick on May 1, 1786, was physically able and mentally *capable* of drafting, signing and promulgating these Grand Constitutions, we have utterly failed to find that he discovered or pointed out to us one scintilla of evidence that Frederick actually did have aught to do with them."[12]

Pike was obviously aware that his lengthy account did not answer the actual question of whether Frederic signed or approved the Grand Constitutions. Addressing this point in a most interesting manner, Pike writes:

> "[T]here is not one particle of proof, of any sort, circumstantial or historical or by argument from improbability, that they are not genuine and authentic."[13]

As remarkable as it sounds, Pike is actually asking us to prove a negative. Regardless of Pike's request, Baynard goes on to write:

"We conclude therefore:
1. That the Grand Constitutions were not promulgated by Frederic the Great;
2. That they were not framed, drawn up or signed in Berlin;
3. That there did not exist in Berlin or even France in 1786, any "Grand Supreme Universal Inspectors, in constituted Supreme Council";

4. That the real date of the Constitutions is subsequent to 1786."[14]

But if the Grand Constitutions are a forgery, then who forged them? The question did not escape Baynard:

"It is only natural that the next question should be, Well, then, who did frame them? We do not know. Neither are we unduly disturbed because we do not know. We have our opinion, but it is not substantiated by any evidence that we can call positive or direct, and, therefore, we do not express it as a conclusion."[15]

To summarize the situation, Pike had already proclaimed the French version of the Grand Constitutions a forgery. He was debating the merits of why the Latin version should be considered legitimate. Baynard rejected *both* versions of the Grand Constitutions. Regarding the possibility that the Latin version might also be a forgery, Pike tells us:

"The odious charge has been again and again repeated, that these Latin Constitutions were forged at Charleston. It is quite certain that this is not true, because the Supreme Council at Charleston never had them, until it received copies of the editions published by the Grand Commander. If they were forged anywhere, it was not at Charleston: and if anything was forged there, it was the French copy, as it afterwards appeared in the *Recueil des Actes*."[16]

And elsewhere:

"The gentlemen of South Carolina, in that day, did not commit forgery. Whatever the origin of the Grand Constitutions, they came from Europe to Charleston, and were accepted and received by the honorable gentlemen and clergymen who were of the first Supreme Council, in perfect good faith"[17]

If the Grand Constitutions are forged documents, but the original Charleston Council did not forge them, then how did they come into possession of them? Pike theorizes:

> "This very imperfect French copy, which consists merely of so many Articles, without preface, formality of enactment by any body in Power, or authentication of any sort, contains no list of the degrees, nor even the name of the Rite. It is most probable that de Grasse procured it, in or from Europe, and created the Supreme Council. By Article V of these Constitutions, it requires three persons to constitute a quorum and compose a Supreme Council; and therefore Colonel Mitchell and Dr. Dalcho alone could not have been, by themselves, such a body. Brother de Grasse intended establishing a Supreme Council at Santo Domingo for the French West India Islands; and no other person had any interest to make the Constitutions read so as to allow such a Council, except his father-in-law, Jean Baptiste Delahogue, who also resided in Charleston in 1796, 1799 and 1801, and was also a 33rd, and appointed to be Lieutenant Grand Commander for the French West Indies. It was for this reason, evidently, that neither of them was placed on the roll of members of the body at Charleston."[18]

We now have enough material to analyze. Baynard held the opinion that the entire story of the Grand Constitutions was a fabrication. He based his opinion on the total lack of factual evidence supporting the account and the improbability of the reported events. Pike soundly denounced the French version as a fraud, but held to the possibility of legitimacy for the Latin version. Pike pointed out that the original Charleston Council did not have possession or knowledge of the Latin version and had based their actions on the fraudulent French version. Pike also stated that it was Alexander de Grasse-Tilly who had brought the forged French version to Charleston, and implied that it was de Grasse-Tilly who might actually have forged them. Pike, with some indignation, rejected the possibility that Mitchell or Dalcho might have had anything to do with forgery.

There are two logical scenarios that we can explore: The first would be that Mitchell and Dalcho received the Grand Constitutions sincerely believing they were legitimate; the second would be that Mitchell and Dalcho took part in the creation of the Grand Constitutions or knew that they were a forgery.

If Mitchell and Dalcho believed that the Grand Constitutions were legitimate, we can look at the series of events with this mindset. If Mitchell and Dalcho believed that they were propagating a European system created some 15 years prior to the creation of the Charleston Council, then they could have reasonably assumed that other Supreme Councils of the 33° existed in Europe. Clearly, the Grand Constitutions speak of such a Council in Berlin.

On August 23, 1813 John Mitchell and Frederick Dalcho wrote to Emanuel de la Motta concerning de la Motta's report to them of Cerneau. Mitchell wrote in part:

"I am truly surprised and astonished at the conduct of the man you say is called Mr. Joseph Cerneau. No person ever had the degree but the Count de Grasse, and perhaps, but I am not sure, Mr. Delahogue."[19]

We must stop for a moment to try and understand this comment by Mitchell. If Mitchell received a copy of the Grand Constitutions and he accepted them as legitimate and authoritative, how could he be so sure that no one else "had the degree"? What of the Supreme Council in Berlin mentioned in the Grand Constitutions? The copy of the Grand Constitutions of 1786 that Mitchell had available to him opens as follows:

"Made and approved in the Supreme Council of the 33rd duly and lawfully established and Congregated in the Grand East of Berlin on the 1st of May Anno Lucis 5786 and of the Christian Era 1786. At which Council was present in person – His Most August Majesty, Frederic 2nd, King of Prussia, Sovereign Grand Commander."

Was the "Supreme Council of the 33rd" in Berlin composed of members who did not have the 33rd degree? If no one else had the degree, who gave it to Mitchell – someone who did not possess it

himself? Mitchell writes that de Grasse was the only other person whom he was certain "had" the degree. (This is possibly where Pike conceived the theory that de Grasse was the one who brought the forged copy to the United States.) If no one else had the degree before de Grasse, then who gave it to de Grasse? If de Grasse gave Mitchell the 33rd at some time earlier than the creation of the Charleston Council in 1801, why does the "1802 Manifesto" (the "birth certificate" of the SJ) state that de Grasse received the 33° from Mitchell on the "21st of February, 5802" [1802]? [20]

Let's now look at part of the letter Frederick Dalcho wrote to de la Motta on the same day as Mitchell's letter and also concerning the new Cerneau creation. It again should be noted that the date of Dalcho's letter was August 23, 1813. Emanuel de la Motta established the Supreme Council for the Northern Jurisdiction 13 days earlier on August 10, 1813, and he certainly would have been reported this fact to Mitchell and Dalcho in the letter that prompted their response. Dalcho wrote:

> "It is well known to those who have lawfully received the 33rd degree, that there can be but one Council in a nation or kingdom; and that the Council for the U.S. was lawfully established in this City, May 31st, 1801; consequently any other assuming its prerogatives must be surreptitious."[21]

What does Dalcho mean by this statement? The copy of the Grand Constitutions of 1786 which exists *in his own hand* says that there "shall" be two in the United States. And what of de la Motta's creation? Is there some suggestion that Dalcho might not have approved of the de la Motta Council any more than the Cerneau one? The "birth certificate" of the NMJ, created by de la Motta, states that "there shall be two Grand & Supreme Councils of the 33d Degree for the Jurisdiction of the United States of America, one for the South and the other for the North."

Pike stated that the earliest known copy of the Grand Constitutions was the "forged" French version as appeared in a French Masonic publication titled *Recueil des Actes* in 1817. [22] Pike stated that Mitchell and Dalcho could not have forged the Constitutions because they were both "honorable" men and neither "the kind of man to put his hand to that kind of work." Pike also stated that it was not "probable that either of them could write

Latin or French." [23] Pike theorized that de Grasse along with his father-in-law, Jean Baptiste Delahogue, acquired or forged the French version and then, presumably, translated it into English so that Mitchell and Dalcho could understand it. Pike did not know of the handwritten Dalcho copy, but could have, by this line of reasoning, assumed that Dalcho copied it from a de Grasse or Delahogue copy which they had translated from French into English.

Could this be the copy that was used to fool Mitchell and Dalcho? We learn from past SJ Grand Historian Ray Baker Harris that the Delahogue documents in the Kloss Collection are "an undoubted copy of the Thirty-Third Degree and the Constitution, Statutes and Regulations, in use in Charleston in 1801-1802 when the Supreme Council was established."[24]

Harris also tells us:

"This assumption is further confirmed by a manuscript copy of the same in English, entirely in the handwriting of Frederick Dalcho. It is the English equivalent of Delahogue's French copy. It is believed to have been the Charleston copy from which Delahogue made his translation into French."[25]

Delahogue made his translation into French? But Pike said that the oldest known copy of the Grand Constitutions was the forged French version. In a reproof of this version, Pike rigidly defended Mitchell and Dalcho based on his position that this forged copy came into their hands, presumably through de Grasse and/or Delahouge, and they simply accepted it as legitimate. The "French version" would have had to have been translated from French into English, not the other way around for Pike's argument to be sound. Is there some support for Harris' position that the French Delahouge copy was made from the English Dalcho copy? Yes. Harris tells us that the Delahogue copy of the Grand Constitutions carries the note: "translated from the English by me [Delahogue]."[26]

For Pike's theory to be correct, de Grasse would have translated his forged French Constitutions into English for Mitchell and Dalcho. Dalcho would then have copied that English translation into his own hand. Then, we are asked to believe that de Grasse's father-in-law did not make a French-to-French copy of the Constitutions from de Grasse's copy, but instead used Dalcho's English copy to translate

it back into French for his own personal copy. That makes no sense at all! Why would Delahogue go to all that trouble if his son-in-law possessed the original French version?

This writer is wholly in agreement with Samuel Baynard in his rejection of the legitimacy of the Grand Constitutions. Likewise, there is little room to argue the perfectly logical assessment that Albert Pike made of the French version of the Grand Constitutions. Pike clearly did not realize that what he so soundly proved to be a "clumsy forgery" came directly from the hand of Frederick Dalcho.

In the absence of any other reasonable explanation, we must conclude that John Mitchell and Frederick Dalcho fabricated the story of the Grand Constitutions of 1786, either in whole or in part. We cannot, as Pike suggested, attempt to prove or disprove a negative. We also cannot embrace fanciful theories that make the story end as we might wish. The course of events simply does not make sense if we take the position that Mitchell and Dalcho received the Grand Constitutions, accepted them as legitimate, and created the Charleston Council. The known facts simply do not support such conclusions.

This writer holds the opinion that Mitchell, Dalcho, and possibly a few others held reasonable concern in regard to the failing and chaotic state of the "Scottish Rite" order (Order of the Royal Secret or Rite of Perfection). To bring "order" to the chaos, the new 33-degree AASR system was created. The cream of the crop of the degrees and rituals were selected for this new system, an inspired creation for which, one can imagine, a concern developed over whether it would be accepted by Freemasonry. A royal endorsement would add value to any new Masonic system, and one attached to a set of governing laws might bestow greater value.

If we examine the situation from the standpoint that the Charleston Council received the constitutions and accepted them as legitimate, then we arrive at one contradiction after another. If, however, we consider the entire story and creation came from the Charleston Council, a very logical scenario develops. It is this writer's conclusion that the original Charleston Council was created alongside a set of governing laws attributed to Frederic II. This writer has not seen one scrap of sound evidence to support the position that Frederic actually approved – or even knew of – any Grand Constitutions in Berlin on May 1, 1786. There is, however, abundant

evidence to attribute the creation of the constitutions to the original members of the Charleston Council.

It has been more than 200 years since the creation of the Charleston Council. The value and worth of the AASR is well proven. It is clear this Masonic system is of tremendous importance to the whole of Masonry, and it is not a disservice to acknowledge all of its history. The creators of the AASR were human, after all, and humans sometimes make mistakes in judgment.

NOTES:

1. Albert Pike, *The Grand Constitutions of Freemasonry* (New York: The Supreme Council, 33° Southern Jurisdiction, USA, 1872), 282-283.

2. Henry C. Clausen, *Authentics of Fundamental Law for Scottish Rite Freemasonry* (San Diego: The Supreme Council, 33° Southern Jurisdiction, USA, 1979), 9-10.

3. *Transactions of the Supreme Council of the 33D for the Southern Jurisdiction of the United States* (New York: Masonic Publishing Company, 1869), 19.

4. Ibid., 22-23.

5. Pike, *The Grand Constitutions of Freemasonry* 289. Pike altered the English translation of the French version of Article five to: "...but two in the United States of America..." in order to emphasize his point concerning his interpretation of the meaning of this phrase.

6. Ibid., 283.

7. See Article V, pages 121-123 of this work. In Pike's 1872 (A.M. 5632) *The Grand Constitutions of Freemasonry*, he altered the original translation of the Latin version to read as follows: "In each great nation of Europe, and in each Kingdom or Empire, there shall be a single Council of the said degree. In the States and Provinces, as well on the Continent as in the Islands, whereof North America consists, there will be two Councils, one at as great a distance from the other as may be possible." Pike, the master linguist, replaced the word "shall" with "will" in his 1872 edition, which, while having the same meaning, was not such an obvious problem to inattentive readers. The edited edition carries the note, "Re-translated from the Latin by Albert Pike, 33°, Sov. Gr. Commander. A.M., 5632" p. 213. Pike maintained the accuracy of his 1859 translation, at least, until 1868, as the questioned portion of Article Five is reproduced in the 1868 *Transactions* of the SC SJ exactly as they appeared in the 1859 translation.

8. Samuel Harrison Baynard, Jr., *History of the Supreme Council, 33° Ancient and Accepted Scottish Rite Northern Masonic Jurisdiction of the United States of America and its Antecedents* (Boston: The Supreme Council, 33° Northern Masonic Jurisdiction, USA, 1938), Vol. I, 175-179. This quotation is taken from the

facsimile reproduction of the 1813 "birth certificate" for the Northern Jurisdiction (reproduced on page 176). In addition to the facsimile is a printed transcript of the "birth certificate" provided to us by Ill. Brother Baynard. Interestingly, the printed transcription omits a number of words and phrases that appear in the facsimile. The phrase, for example, "one for the South and one for the North" (line 26 of the facsimile), does not appear in the printed transcription.

9. The question of where and when John Mitchell and Joseph Cerneau received their 33rd degrees has not escaped the notice of Masonic researchers. In the case of Cerneau, he is usually dismissed quickly due to the total lack of evidence that anyone ever actually gave him the 33rd degree. Emanuel de la Motta, upon first meeting Cerneau, attempted to obtain certain information about Cerneau's 33rd including having a look at his Patent, but was unable to satisfy himself in any way (see: Charles S. Lobingier, *The Supreme Council 33°* [Louisville, Kentucky: The Supreme Council, 33°, SJ., 1964], p. 102.). But what of John Mitchell? There has never been a Patent discovered showing that Mitchell received the 33rd from anyone. We know that Mitchell gave Dalcho the 33rd as a Patent for this event exists. Mitchell was the first Sovereign Grand Commander of the SJ, so how did he receive the 33rd? Who gave it to him? Prior to Mitchell's role in the creation of the AASR, he was a Deputy Inspector General (25°) of the so-called "Rite of Perfection". We often see those senior to Mitchell in this system being credited with giving him the 33rd (usually Barend Spitzer). How could a 25th degree Mason from another system give the 33rd degree of the AASR to someone? We can also see an account of some "unknown" Prussian or German giving him the degree with Mitchell signing an obligation for it *in French*. (See: Baynard, *History of the Supreme Council, 33°*, Vol. 1, p. 89.) If someone gave Mitchell the 33rd, who gave it to *him*? Why didn't this unknown SGIG play a role in the creation of the Charleston Council? Since this unknown SGIG was senior to Mitchell, why wasn't *he* the first Charleston Sovereign Grand Commander? The questions can go on forever.

One thing we must never do is judge past events by today's standards. How we do things today, may not have been the norm in the past. We can find evidence of an old practice that might shed some light on the Mitchell/Cerneau 33rd degree question. Evidence exists (see: Henry Wilson Coil, *Coil's Masonic Encyclopedia* [New York: Macoy Pub. & Masonic Supply Co., 1961], p. 121 and Pike, *The Grand Constitutions of Freemasonry*, p. 117.) that a Deputy Inspector General of the old so-called "Rite of Perfection" (as were both Mitchell and Cerneau) could "slide over" to the 32nd degree of the new 33 degree AASR. In addition, if a 32nd of the AASR was the senior (or only) 32nd in an unoccupied area, he could advance himself to the 33rd degree of the AASR in order to give the degree to others and create a Supreme Council. Both Mitchell and Cerneau gave the 33rd to others and created supreme councils.

Regardless of the historic disapproval of Cerneau, it is possible that according to the custom of that time, he received the 33rd degree in the same manner as did Mitchell. A sound argument could be made that he was just as legitimate a SGIG as was Mitchell.

10. See: R. Baker Harris and James D. Carter, *History of the Supreme Council, 33° (1801-1861)* (Washington, D.C.: The Supreme Council, 33° Southern Jurisdiction, USA, 1964), 98.

11. Ibid., 216.

12. Baynard, *History of the Supreme Council, 33°*, 101.

13. Pike, *The Grand Constitutions of Freemasonry*, 170.

14. Baynard, *History of the Supreme Council, 33°*, 115.

15. Ibid., 116.

16. Pike, *The Grand Constitutions of Freemasonry* 126.

17. Ibid., 195.

18. Ibid., 134.

19. Harris/Carter, *History of the Supreme Council, 33° (1801-1861)*, 117.

20. Ibid., 323.

21. Ibid., 118.

22. Pike, *The Grand Constitutions of Freemasonry,* 126.

23. Ibid., 134.

24. Harris/Carter, *History of the Supreme Council, 33° (1801-1861)*, 92.

25. Ibid., 92.

26. Ibid., 92.

THE

STATUTES AND REGULATIONS,

INSTITUTES, LAWS

AND

GRAND CONSTITUTIONS

OF THE

𝕬𝖓𝖈𝖎𝖊𝖓𝖙 𝖆𝖓𝖉 𝕬𝖈𝖈𝖊𝖕𝖙𝖊𝖉 𝕾𝖈𝖔𝖙𝖙𝖎𝖘𝖍 𝕽𝖎𝖙𝖊.

COMPILED, WITH NOTES, FROM AUTHENTIC DOCUMENTS,

FOR THE USE OF THE ORDER.

BY ALBERT PIKE, 33d,

M.˙. P.˙. SOVEREIGN GRAND COMMANDER OF THE SUPREME COUNCIL FOR THE SOUTHERN JURISDICTION
OF THE UNITED STATES.

1859

Grand Orient of Charleston, So: Car:.

3ᵈ day of Sisri, A∴ M∴ 5620.

I, Albert Pike, Sov∴ Grand Comman-
der of the Supreme Council of Sov∴ Gr∴ Insprs∴
Genl∴ of the 33ᵈ Degree for the Southern Jurisdiction of the United States, do hereby certify.
That the foregoing Constitutions and Regulations
in French, of the year 1762, with the Statutes,
Regulations, Institutes and Balustres that
follow have been accurately copied by me from
the ancient manuscripts in the archives of
the Supreme Council at Charleston; and the
same have been carefully translated by me;
that the foregoing Constitutions of 1786 are an
accurate copy in Latin, of the copy authenticated in 1834 by the Supreme Councils of France
and Brazil and which copy is recognized
by the Supreme Council at Charleston as
:authentic: that the same has been care-

fully translated into English by me: and that
the foregoing new Statutes of the Supreme
Council for the Southern Jurisdiction of the
United States were adopted by it at its Session which commenced on the 25th day
of March, A∴ D∴ 1859; and that they,
with the Constitutions, Regulations and
Statutes aforesaid, constitute the law
of the Ancient and Accepted Rite for the
said Southern Jurisdiction

      In witness whereof, I do here-
unto affix the Seal of my arms, at
the Orient aforesaid, this third day of
the Hebrew month תשרי, A∴ M∴ 5620,
answering unto the first day of October, A∴
D∴ 1859

           Albert Pike, 33∴
        Sov∴ Gr∴ Commander &c.

Countersigned
  Albert G. Mackey, 33∴
     Secretary General Holy Empire

INTRODUCTION.

THORY : 1 *Acta Lat.* 79 : 1762, 21 *September.* "Committees from the Council of Emperors of the East and West, at Paris, and the Council of Princes of the Royal Secret, framed, at Bordeaux, the Regulations of the Masonry of Perfection, in thirty-five Articles, and fixed the degrees administered by the Council."

Copies of the CONSTITUTIONS and REGULATIONS of 1762, and of divers subsequent Statutes and Institutes of unknown date and uncertain authenticity, are given in the "*Recueil des Actes du Suprême Conseil de France,*" printed at Paris in 1832, by authority of that body.

In the archives of the Supreme Council at Charleston is a book, in manuscript, written by the Bro.·. JEAN BAPTISTE MARIE DELA-HOGUE himself, in 1798 and 1799; containing, among other docu-ments, a copy of those Constitutions and Regulations, and of other Statutes and Regulations; all authenticated by his genuine signa-ture and that of the Bro.·. Count ALEXANDRE FRANÇOIS AUGUSTE DE GRASSE; under the seal of the Sublime Grand Council of the Princes of the Royal Secret, then in existence, and sitting at Charleston.

There is also in those archives another book, being the Register delivered by the Bro.·. JEAN BAPTISTE AVEILHÉ, Deputy Grand Inspector General and Prince Mason, to the Bro.·. PIERRE DUPONT DELORME, Dep.·. Gr.·. Ins.·. Gen.·. and Prince Mason, at Port-au-Prince, in the Island of Santo Domingo, on the 10th of December, 1797, containing the same and other documents. In this book

2

there is attached to each document a copy of the certificate that they are correct copies, of the Bros∴ HYMAN ISAAC LONG, JEAN BAPTISTE MARIE DELAHOGUE, AUGUSTE DE GRASSE, DOMINIQUE SAINT-PAUL, ALEXIS CLAUDE ROBIN and REMY VICTOR PETIT, Dep∴ Insp∴ Gen∴ and Prince Masons, given at Charleston, on the 9th of June, 1797 ; with the certificate of Bro∴ AVEILHÉ, dated 10th December, 1797 ; and each is *visé* by the Bro∴ DE GRASSE, as Sov∴ Ins∴ Gen∴ 33d degree, on the 12th March, 1802.

In the copies in this latter book there are many obvious errors ; but in substance they agree with those more accurately made by the Bro∴ DELAHOGUE. The copies in the *Recueil des Actes* differ in many respects from both. Some of the variations are evidently caused by alterations purposely made, of later date.

The copy in the *Recueil des Actes* is the later one. That by the Bro∴ DELAHOGUE is a copy of a copy delivered in 1768 by the Bro∴ STEPHEN MORIN to the Bro∴ HENRY A. FRANCKEN, and is evidently the most authentic.

We therefore lay before the reader the original French of these Constitutions and Regulations, and of the other Statutes, according to this earlier copy, with an accurate translation ; remarking only, that even in this copy there are some obvious mistakes, which, how-ever, it is not in our power to correct. Even errors in grammar we have left uncorrected, our object being to give a *literal* copy of each document, even preserving the faulty or antique orthography, from the old manuscripts in the Archives at Charleston.

Constitutions of 1762.

CONSTITUTIONS ET RÈGLEMENS

RÉDIGÉS

PAR NEUF COMMISSAIRES NOMMÉS AD HOC,

PAR

LE SOUVERAIN GRAND CONSEIL SUBLIME

DES

SUBLIMES PRINCES DU ROYAL SECRET, Etc., Etc., Etc.

ORIENTS DE PARIS ET BERLIN.

———

CONSTITUTIONS et RÉGLEMENS rédigés par neuf commissaires nommés par le Grand Conseil des Souverains Princes du Royal Secret, aux Grands Orients de Paris et Berlin, en vertu de la délibération du 5e jour de la 3e semaine, de la 7e Lune de l'Ere Hébraïque, 5562, et de l'Ere Chrétienne, 1762. Pour être ratifiés et observés par les Grands Conseils des Sublimes Chevaliers et Princes de la Maçonnerie, ainsi que par les Conseils particuliers et Grands Inspecteurs régulièrement constitués sur les deux Hémisphères.*

IL est connu que toutes les sociétés ont reçus des grands bienfaits par les travaux constants des Sublimes Chevaliers et Princes de la Maçonnerie ; il ne peut conséquemment être pris trop de précaution et de soins pour soutenir sa dignité, perpétuer ses bonnes maximes, et les préserver des abus qui peuvent s'y introduire.

Quoique cet Ordre Royal et Sublime se soit toujours soutenu avec gloire et applaudissements, par la sagesse et la prudence de ses Constitutions Secrètes, aussi anciennes que le monde, la dépravation

---

* Dans la copie du Fr.·. Aveilhé, le document jusqu'à l'astérisque se lit comme suit :

RÈGLEMENS ET CONSTITUTIONS

Faits par les neuf Commissaires, nommés par le Souverain Grand Conseil des Sublimes Chevaliers du Royal Secret et Princes de la Maçonnerie.

AU GRAND ORIENT DE BORDEAUX, en conséquence de la délibération du 5e jour de la 3e semaine, de la 7e lune de l'Ere Hébraïque, 5562, ou de l'Ere Chrétienne, 1762, pour être observés et ratifiés par ledit Souverain Grand Conseil des Sublimes Chevaliers du Royal Secret, Princes de la Maçonnerie, et par tous les Conseils particuliers régulièrement constitués sur les deux Hémisphères ; transmis à notre frère ETIENNE MORIN, Grand Inspecteur de toutes les Loges dans le Nouveau-Monde, &c.

CONSTITUTIONS AND REGULATIONS

DRAWN UP

BY NINE COMMISSIONERS APPOINTED AD HOC,

BY THE

SOVEREIGN GRAND SUBLIME COUNCIL

OF THE

SUBLIME PRINCES OF THE ROYAL SECRET, Etc., Etc., Etc.

ORIENTS OF PARIS AND BERLIN.

CONSTITUTIONS *and* REGULATIONS *drawn up by nine Commissioners appointed by the Grand Council of the Sovereign Princes of the Royal Secret, at the Grand Orients of Paris and Berlin, by virtue of the resolution of the 5th day of the 3d week of the seventh Month of the Hebrew Era, 5562, and of the Christian Era, 1762. To be ratified and observed by the Grand Councils of the Sublime Knights and Princes of Masonry, as well as by the particular Councils and Grand Inspectors regularly constituted in the two Hemispheres.* *

IT is known that all the associations have been greatly benefited by the assiduous labors of the Sublime Knights and Princes of Masonry; and therefore too much precaution and pains cannot be taken to preserve unimpaired its dignity, to perpetuate its excellent maxims, and to preserve them from those abuses that ever seek to obtain foothold.

Although this Royal and Sublime Order has always sustained itself in honor and credit, by the wisdom and prudence of its Secret Constitutions, as ancient as the world; the depravation of the

---

* In *Aveilhé's* copy, the document, to the asterisk, reads thus :
REGULATIONS AND CONSTITUTIONS
Made by the Nine Commissioners appointed by the Sovereign Grand Council of the Sublime Knights of the Royal Secret and Princes of Masonry.

AT THE GRAND ORIENT OF BORDEAUX, in consequence of the resolution of the 5th day of the 3d week of the 7th month, of the Hebrew Era, 5562, or of the Christian Era, 1762, to be observed and ratified by the said Sovereign Grand Council of the Sublime Knights of the Royal Secret, Princes of Masonry, and by all the particular Councils regularly constituted over the two Hemispheres : transmitted to our Bro.·. STEPHEN MORIN, Grand Inspector of all the Lodges in the New World, &c.

du siècle présent a rendu nécessaire et convenable d'y faire des réformes convenables et conformes aux temps où nous vivons.

La manière de vivre de nos premiers Patriarches qui avaient été naturalisés et élevés dans le sein de la Perfection, présente un tableau bien différent des mœurs actuelles. Dans ces temps heureux, la Pureté, l'Innocence et la Candeur guidaient naturellement le cœur vers la Justice et la Perfection; mais la dépravation des mœurs, occasionnée par les déréglements du cœur et de l'esprit, ayant, par succession des temps détruite toutes les vertus; l'Innocence et la Candeur qui en sont la base, ont insensiblement disparues, et laissées l'espèce humaine abandonnée aux horreurs de la misère, de l'injustice et de l'imperfection.

Cependant ce vice n'a pas été général parmi nos Vénérables Patriarches; nos premiers Chevaliers ont échappés à la multitude des écueils qui les menaçaient du naufrage; ils se sont maintenus dans cet heureux état d'innocence, de justice et de perfection qu'ils ont heureusement transmis d'âge en âge à leur postérité, en ne révélant les sacrés mystères qu'à ceux qu'ils en jugeaient dignes, et auxquels l'Eternel nous a permis de participer.

En conséquence, pour nous maintenir, ainsi que tous nos Sublimes Chevaliers et Princes de la Maçonnerie Sublime, nos Frères, dans cet heureux état, et de leur avis, il a été arrêté, conclu et déterminé qu'outre les Anciennes et Secrètes Constitutions de l'Ordre Auguste des Sublimes Princes de la Maçonnerie, et pour être à jamais entièrement et religieusement observé, que les grades sublimes ne seront jamais communiqués aux Maçons au-dessous des grades de *Chevalier d'Orient*, de *Princes de Jérusalem*, *Chevalier d'Orient et d'Occident*, *Patriarche Noachite*, *Chevalier du Royal Arche*, *Prince Adepte, et Commandeur de l'Aigle blanc et noir;* pour, par cette précaution, s'assurer s'ils possèdent les qualités nécessaires pour être admis auxdits grades sublimes.

Lesdites Constitutions et Règlemens doivent être exactement exécutés et observés dans tous les points et articles, comme suit :

ARTICLE I.

Comme la Religion est un culte nécessairement dû au Dieu Tout-Puissant, nulle personne ne sera initié dans les mystères sacrés de cet éminent grade, s'il n'est pas soumis aux devoirs de la religion

present age makes it necessary and proper to make therein such reformatory alterations as are suitable and fitting to the times in which we live.

The mode of life of our first Patriarchs, who were created and reared in the bosom of Perfection, presents a very different picture from that of our modern manners. In those fortunate times, Purity, Innocence, and Candour naturally led the heart towards Justice and Perfection; but the depravation of morals, caused by the irregularities of the heart and intellect, having in process of time destroyed all the virtues; Innocence and Candour, which are their basis, insensibly disappeared, and left the human race a prey to the horrors of misery, injustice and imperfection.

But, nevertheless, vice did not generally prevail among our Venerable Patriarchs: our first Knights avoided the multitude of shoals that threatened them with shipwreck; they maintained themselves in that happy condition of innocence, justice and perfection which they fortunately transmitted to their posterity from age to age, revealing the sacred mysteries to those only whom they judged worthy; into which mysteries the Eternal has been pleased to allow us to be initiated.

Consequently, in order to maintain ourselves, as well as all our Sublime Knights and Princes of the Sublime Masonry, our Brethren, in that happy state and condition, and by their advice, it has been resolved, settled and determined, that, in addition to the Ancient and Secret Constitutions of the August Order of the Sublime Princes of Masonry, and as a rule to be forever punctually and religiously observed, the Sublime degrees shall be never communicated to Masons below the degrees of *Knight of the East,* of *Princes of Jerusalem, Knight of the East and West, Patriarch Noachite, Knight of the Royal Arch, Prince Adept,* and *Commander of the White and Black Eagle:* To the end that by this precaution it may be made certain that they do possess the qualities necessary to warrant admission to the said Sublime degrees.

The said Constitutions and Regulations are to be punctually executed and observed, in all their points and articles, as follows:

ARTICLE I.

FORASMUCH as Religion is a worship necessarily due to the Omnipotent God, no person shall be initiated into the Sacred Mysteries of this eminent degree, unless he complies with what is required of

du pays où il doit indispensablement en avoir reçu les vénérables principes ; et que cela soit certifié par trois Chevaliers, Princes Maçons ; qu'il soit né de parents libres ; qu'il a mené une bonne conduite, jouit d'une bonne réputation, et a été admis comme tel dans tous les précédents grades de la Maçonnerie ; et qu'il a, en tout temps, donné des preuves d'obéissance, soumission, zèle, ferveur et constance ; et qu'enfin il est libre de contracter les obligations de la Vénérable Maçonnerie Sublime, lorsqu'il sera admis au sublime grade de la Haute Perfection, comme aussi d'obéir avec exactitude au Très Ill.˙. Souverain, Grand Commandeur, ses Officiers, et au Souverain et Puissant Grand Conseil des Sublimes Princes assemblés.

ARTICLE II.

L'Art Royal ou la Société des Maçons Libres et Acceptés est divisé par ordre, en 25 grades connus. Le 1er est inférieur au 2d ; le 2d au 3e, et ainsi de suite, par progression successive, jusqu'au 25e, qui est le Sublime et dernier qui gouverne et commande tous les autres sans exception. Tous ces grades sont divisés en 7 classes, par lesquelles on ne peut être dispensé de passer, ni de suivre exactement l'ordre des temps et les distances entre chaque grade, divisés par nombres mystérieux, comme suit :

1re Classe : 3 Grades.	1. Pour parvenir à l'Apprentif,	3 mois.
	2. De l'Apprentif au Compagnon,	5 "
	3. Du Compagnon au Maître,	7 "
		15 mois.. 3 × 5.
2de Classe : 5 Grades.	4. Du Maître au Maître Secret,	3 "
	5. Du Maître Secret au Maître Parfait,	3 "
	6. Du Maître Parfait au Secrétaire Intime,	3 "
	7. Du Secrétaire Intime au Prévôt et Juge,*	5 "
	8. Du Prévôt et Juge à l'Intendant des Bâtiments,*	7 "
		21 mois.

* Here I have corrected an evident error. The Text makes the *Prévôt et Juge* the 8th degree, and *l'Intendant des bâtiments* the 7th. The 9th degree in the text is correct, and shows the error.

him by the religion of his country, where he must necessarily have imbibed its venerable principles; nor unless that is certified by three Knights, Princes Masons; nor unless he is of free parents; nor unless he has conducted himself well, and is under the tongue of good report, and has, as such, been admitted in all the preceding degrees of Masonry; nor unless he has at all times given proofs of his obedience, docility, zeal, fervour and constancy; nor, finally, unless he is free to take upon himself the obligations of Venerable Sublime Masonry, when admitted to the sublime degree of High Perfection, and also free punctually to obey the Th∴ Ill∴ Sovereign Grand Commander, his Officers, and the Sovereign and Puissant Grand Council, of the Sublime Princes, when assembled.

ARTICLE II.

The Royal Art, or the Association of Free and Accepted Masons, is regularly divided into 25 known degrees. The first is below the second, the second below the third, and so on in successive progression to the 25th, which is the Sublime, and last, that governs and commands all the others without exception. The whole of the degrees are divided into seven classes, through which no one can be excused from passing, nor from observing punctually the order of times and the distances fixed between the degrees, divided by mysterious numbers, as follows:

1st Class:
3 Degrees.

1. To attain the degree of Apprentice, 3 mos.
2. From Apprentice to Fellow-Craft, 5 "
3. From Fellow-Craft to Master, 7 "

15 mos...3×5

2d Class:
5 Degrees.

4. From Master to Secret Master, 3 "
5. From Secret Master to Perfect Master, 3 "
6. From Perfect Master to Confidential Secretary, 3 "
7. From Confidential Secretary to Provost and Judge, 5 "
8. From Provost and Judge to Intendant of the Buildings, 7 "

21 mos.

3me Classe : 3 Grades.	9. De l'Intendant des Bâtiments à l'Elu des 9,	3 mois.
	10. De l'Elu des 9 à l'Elu des 15,	3 "
	11. De l'Elu des 15 à l'Elu Illustre, Chef des 12 Tribus,	1 "
		7 mois.

4me Classe : 3 Grades.	12. De l'Elu Illustre au Grand Maître Architecte,	1 "
	13. Du G'd M'e Arc'te au Chev. du Royal Arche,	3 "
	14. Du Chev. du Royal Arche au G'd Elu Anc. M'e Parfait ou Perfection,	1 "
		5 mois.

5me Classe ; 4 Grades.	15. De la Perfection au Chev. d'O. ou de l'Epée,	1 "
	16. Du Chev. d'Orient au Prince de Jérusalem,	1 "
	17. Du Prince de Jérusalem au Ch. d'Orient et d'Occident,	3 "
	18. Du Ch. d'Orient et d'Occident au Ch. de Rose Croix,	1 "
		6 mois.

6me Classe ; 4 Grades.	19. Du Chev. de Rose Croix au Gr. Pontif ou M'e *ad vitam*,	3 "
	20. Du Gr.·. Pontif au Gr.·. Patriarche Noachite,	3 "
	21. Du Gr.·. Patriarche Noachite au Gr.·. M'e de la Clef de la Maçonnerie,	3 "
	22. De la Clef de M'ie au Prince de Liban ou Royale Hache,	3 "
		12 mois.

3d Class: 3 Degrees.	9. From Intendent of the Buildings to the Elect of the 9,	3 mos.
	10. From the Elect of the 9 to the Elect of the 15,	3 "
	11. From the Elect of the 15 to the Ill.·. Elect, Chief of the Tribes,	1 "
		7 mos.

4th Class: 3 Degrees.	12. From the Ill.·. Elect to the Gr.·. Master Architect,	1 "
	13. From the Gr.·. M.·. Architect to the Kt.·. of the Royal Arch,	3 "
	14. From the Kt.·. of R.·. A.·. to the Gr.·. Elect Ancient, Perfect Master, or Perfection,	1 "
		5 mos.

5th Class: 4 Degrees.	15. From Perfection to the Kt.·. of the East or of the Sword,	1 "
	16. From Kt.·. of the East to Prince of Jerusalem,	1 "
	17. From Pr.·. of Jerusalem to Kt.·. of the East and West,	3 "
	18. From Kt.·. of the East and West to Kt.·. of Rose Croix,	1 "
		6 mos.

6th Class: 4 Degrees.	19. From Kt.·. of Rose Croix to Gr.·. Pontiff or Master ad vitam,	3 "
	20. From Gr.·. Pontiff to Gr.·. Patriarch Noachite,	3 "
	21. From Gr.·. Patriarch Noachite to Gr.·. Master of the Key of Masonry,	3 "
	22. From the Key of Masonry to Prince of Libanus or Royal Axe,	3 "
		12 mos.

<table>
<tr><td rowspan="5">7me Classe :
3 Grades.</td><td>23. De Roy. Hache au Sov. Prince</td><td></td></tr>
<tr><td>Adepte,</td><td>5 mois.</td></tr>
<tr><td>24. Du Pr. Adepte à l'Ill. Chev.</td><td></td></tr>
<tr><td>Com. de l'Aigle Blanc et Noir,</td><td>5 "</td></tr>
<tr><td>25. Du Ch. de l'Aigle Blanc et Noir</td><td></td></tr>
</table>

25. Du Ch. de l'Aigle Blanc et Noir
    au Sub. Pr. du Roy. Secret,   5 "
                                  ———
                                  15 mois.

Tous ces grades, auxquels on ne peut être initié que dans un nombre mystérieux de mois, pour parvenir à chaque grade suivant, forment le nombre de 81 mois ;* mais si dans un temps un Frère avait manqué au zèle et à l'obéissance, il ne pourroit obtenir aucuns grades, jusqu'à ce qu'il eût fait ses soumissions, imploré le pardon de sa faute, et promis la plus grande exactitude et une soumission exemplaire, sous peine d'être exclus à perpétuité et d'avoir son nom biffé et rayé de la liste des vrais et légitimes frères, &c.

ARTICLE III.

Le Souverain Conseil des Princes Sublimes est composé de tous les Présidents des Conseils, particulièrement et régulièrement constitués dans les villes de Paris et Bordeaux ; le Souverain des Souverains ou son Député Général ou son Représentant à leur tête.

ARTICLE IV.

Le Souverain Grand Conseil des Sublimes Princes du Royal Secret s'assemblera quatre fois par an, et sera appelé Grand Conseil de Quartier de Communication, qui sera tenu les 25 Juin, 21 Septembre, 21 Mars, et 27 Décembre.

ARTICLE V.†

Le 25 Juin, le Souverain Grand Conseil sera composé de tous

---

* In Aveilbé's copy, this paragraph, to the asterisk, reads thus, (as it does in the *Recueil des Actes*):

"Tous ces grades dans lesquels il faut être initié dans un nombre mystérieux de mois, pour arriver successivement à chaque grade suivant, forment le nombre de quatre-vingt un mois. 8 et 1 font 9, comme 8 et 1 font 81, comme 9 fois 9 font 81, tous nombres parfaits. Bien différent, 1 et 8 qui font 9, comme 1 et 8 font 18, comme 2 fois 9 font 18. Car il y a des nombres imparfaits, et cette combinaison est épineuse et difficile ; mais un Franc-Maçon qui a rempli son temps, cueille enfin la Rose Maçonnique."

† This Article, wholly omitted in the certified and sealed copy of Delahogue and de Grasse, is supplied from Aveilhé's copy, agreeing with the *Recueil des Actes*.

7th Class.
{
23. From Royal Axe to Sov.∴ Prince
    Adept,   5 mos.
24. From Prince Adept to the Ill.∴.
    Kt.∴. Commander of the White
    and Black Eagle,   5 "
25. From the Kt.∴. of the White and
    Black Eagle to the Sublime
    Prince of the Royal Secret, 5 "
}

15 mos.

All these degrees, into which one can only be initiated in a mysterious number of months, to arrive at each degree in due succession, make the number, in all, of 81 months;* but if, during any one of the periods, a Bro.∴. has been wanting in zeal and obedience, he can obtain no more degrees, until he has submitted to discipline, implored pardon for his fault, and promised the utmost punctuality and exemplary obedience, under the penalty of being forever excluded, and of having his name erased and struck from the list of true and legitimate brethren, &c., &c., &c.

ARTICLE III.

The Sovereign Grand Council of the Sublime Princes of the Royal Secret is composed of all the Presidents of the several Councils particularly and regularly established, in the cities of Paris and Bordeaux, with the Sovereign of the Sovereigns, or his Deputy General or Representative at their head.

ARTICLE IV.

The Sovereign Grand Council of the Sublime Princes of the Royal Secret shall assemble four times a year, and be styled the Grand Quarterly Council of Communication, held on the 25th of June, the 21st of September, the 21st of March, and the 27th of December.

ARTICLE V.

On the 25th of June, the Sov.∴. Grand Council shall be com-

---

* In *Areilhé's* copy, and the *Recueil des Actes*, this paragraph, to the asterisk, reads thus :
" All these degrees, into which one must be initiated in a mysterious number of months, to arrive at each degree in due succession, form the number of 81 months. 8+1 make 9, as 8 and 1 make 81, and as 9 times 9 make 81, all of which are perfect numbers. Quite otherwise, 1 and 8 make 9, as 1 and 8 make 18, and as twice 9 make 18. For these are imperfect numbers, and this combination is thorny and difficult ; but a Free Mason who has fulfilled his time, at last gathers the Masonic rose."

les Présidents du Conseil, particulièrement * de Paris et de Bordeaux ou de leurs Représentans, pour ce jour seulement, avec leurs deux premiers Grands Officiers, qui sont les Ministres d'Etat et Généraux de l'Armée, qui ont seulement le droit de proposer, sans voix délibérative.

ARTICLE VI.

Tous les 3 ans, le 27 Décembre, le Souverain Grand Conseil nommera 17 Officiers, savoir : 2 Représentants du Lieutenant Commandant, deux Grands Officiers, qui sont le Grand Orateur et le Grand Général de l'Armée, un Grand Garde des Sceaux et Archives, un Secrétaire Général, un Secrétaire pour Paris et Bordeaux, un autre Secrétaire pour les Provinces et Pays Etrangers, un Grand Architecte Ingénieur, un Grand Hospitalier Médecin, et sept Inspecteurs qui se réuniront sous les ordres du Souverain des Souverains Princes ou son Substitut-Général ; composant le nombre de 17, à quoi restera invariablement fixé le nombre des Grands Officiers du Souverain Grand Conseil des Sublimes Princes du Royal Secret, qui ne peuvent être choisis, que parmi les Présidents des Conseils particuliers des Princes de Jérusalem, régulièrement constitués à Paris et Bordeaux ; et à défaut du Souverain et du Sublime Grand Conseil, pour faire les nominations, le Souverain des Souverains Princes ou son Député-Général pourra les nommer d'office, dans un Grand Conseil, assemblé au moins de 18 Princes résidens du Conseil particulièrement † des villes de Paris et Bordeaux.

ARTICLE VII.

Chaque Prince Grand Officier ou Dépositaire [Dignitaire ?] du Souverain Grand Conseil, aura une Patente de la dignité à laquelle il aura été nommé, dans laquelle sera exprimée la durée de ses fonctions, contresignée par tous les Grands Officiers et par ceux du Souverain Grand Conseil des Sublimes Princes, timbrée et scellée.

ARTICLE VIII.

Outre les 4 Assemblées de Communication, il sera tenu tous les mois, dans les premiers 10 jours, par les Grands Officiers, et en di-

---

* *Des Conseils particuliers ?*

† *Sic.* in the original, as in *Aveilhé's* copy and the *Recueil des Actes.* I presume it should read 'des Conseils particuliers.'

posed of all the Presidents of the several Councils of Paris and Bordeaux, or of their Representatives, for that day only, with their two first Grand Officers, the Ministers of State and Generals of the Army, who have only the right to propose measures, but not to vote.

ARTICLE VI.

Every three years, on the 27th of December, the Sovereign Grand Council shall elect 17 officers, to wit: two Representatives of the Lieutenant Commander; two Grand Officers, who are the Grand Orator and the Grand General of the Army; one Grand Keeper of the Seals and Archives; one Secretary General; a Secretary for Paris and Bordeaux; another Secretary for the Provinces and Foreign Countries; a Grand Architect Engineer; a Grand Hospitaller Physician; and 7 Inspectors, who shall meet under the orders of the Sovereign of the Sovereign Princes or his Substitute General; making 17 in all, at which shall remain irrevocably fixed the number of the Grand Officers of the Sovereign Grand Council of the Sublime Princes of the Royal Secret, who can be selected only from among the Presidents of the particular Councils of the Princes of Jerusalem regularly established at Paris and Bordeaux; and upon failure of the Sovereign and the Sublime Grand Council to make the election, the Sovereign of the Sovereign Princes, or his Deputy-General, may, by virtue of his office, appoint the officers, in a Grand Council specially convoked, of at least 18 resident Princes of the particular Councils of the cities of Paris and Bordeaux.

ARTICLE VII.

Every Prince Grand Officer or Dignitary of the Sovereign Grand Council shall have a patent of the dignity to which he shall have been elected, in which shall be expressed the term for which he is elected, countersigned by all the Grand Officers, and by those of the Sovereign Grand Council of the Sublime Princes, and stamped and sealed.

ARTICLE VIII.

Besides the four quarterly communications, there shall be held, within the ten first days of each month, by only the Grand Officers-

gnité du Souverain Conseil des Princes Sublimes seulement, un
Conseil pour régler les affaires de l'Ordre, soit grandes ou particulières, sauf l'appel au Grand. Conseil de Communication.

ARTICLE IX.

Dans l'Assemblée du Conseil de Communication, ainsi que dans
les Conseils particuliers, tout sera décidé à la pluralité des voix. Le
Président aura deux voix et les autres membres une. Si dans ces
Assemblées, un Frère est admis par dispense, quoiqu'il soit Prince
Sublime, sans être membre du Grand Conseil, il n'aura pas de voix,
et ne donnera pas son sentiment sans la permission du Président.

ARTICLE X.

Toutes les affaires portées au Souverain Grand Conseil des Princes
Sublimes seront réglées dans ces Conseils, et ses règlemens seront
exécutés, sauf leur ratification au prochain Conseil de Communication.

ARTICLE XI.

Quand le Souverain Grand Conseil de Communication sera tenu,
le Grand Secrétaire sera obligé d'apporter tous les régistres cou-
rants, et de rendre compte de toutes les délibérations et règlemens
faits pendant le quartier, pour être ratifiés ; et s'il se rencontroit
quelques oppositions à leur ratification, il sera nommé neuf Commissaires, devant lesquels les opposants délivreront par écrit les motifs
de leur opposition, afin qu'il puisse y être pareillement répondu par
écrit, et sur le rapport des susdits commissaires, il en soit arrêté au
Grand Conseil de Communication suivant ; et dans l'intervalle de la
susdite délibération et règlement, il sera exécuté par un ordre.

ARTICLE XII.

Le Grand Secrétaire Général tiendra un régistre pour Paris et
Bordeaux, et un autre pour les Provinces et les Pays Etrangers,
contenant les noms des Conseils Particuliers, par ordre d'ancienneté,
la date de leurs constitutions, l'état de leurs noms, grades et dignités, qualités civiles et résidences des membres, conformément à ceux
envoyés par nos Inspecteurs ou leurs Députés, et le droit de pré-
séance de chaque Conseil, ainsi que le nombre des loges régulières
de Perfection, établies dans le gouvernement des nos Inspecteurs

Dignitaries of the Sovereign Council of the Sublime Princes, a Council for the Regulation of the general and special affairs of the order, with right of appeal to the Grand Council of Communication.

ARTICLE IX.

In the Assembly of the Council of Communication, as also in the particular Councils, all questions shall be decided by plurality of votes; the President having two votes, and each other member one. If a Bro∴ is allowed to sit in such Assembly, by dispensation, even if he be a Sublime Prince, but be not a member of the Grand Council, he shall have no vote, and shall express his views only by permission of the President.

ARTICLE X.

All matters referred to the Sovereign Grand Council of the Sublime Princes shall be determined in the Councils; and their regulations shall be executed, subject to ratification, however, by the next Council of Communication.

ARTICLE XI.

Whenever the Grand Council of Communication is held, the Grand Secretary shall bring up all the current records, and report all the deliberations had, and regulations made during the quarter, that they may be ratified; and if there be any opposition made to such ratification, a Committee of Nine shall be appointed, before which those who object shall set forth in writing the grounds of their objection, that they may be answered in writing; and that, upon the report of the Committee, the matter may be settled in the next Grand Council of Communication; and in the interval between such deliberation and the final decision that to which objection is made shall, by a mandate, be carried into effect.

ARTICLE XII.

The Grand Secretary-General shall keep a Register for Paris and Bordeaux, and another for the Provinces and Foreign Countries, containing the names of the Subordinate Councils, in the order of their seniority, the dates of their charters, and a statement of the names, degrees, dignities, civil conditions and places of residence of their members, conformably to the forms transmitted by our Inspectors or their deputies; and of the right of precedency of each Council; and also the number of regular Lodges of Perfection

3

ou du Conseil des Princes Sublimes, les titres de leurs Loges, la date de leurs Constitutions, état de leurs titres, grades, offices, dignités, qualités civiles, et les résidences des membres, conformément à ceux qui nous seront délivrés par nos Inspecteurs ou leurs Députés.

Dans les Grands Conseils de Communication sera réglé le jour de la réception du Président, dans les Conseils Particuliers.

ARTICLE XIII.

Le Grand Secrétaire tiendra pareillement un régistre contenant toutes les délibérations et règlemens faits par le Grand Conseil de Communication de quartier, dans lequel seront mentionnées toutes les affaires expédiées dans les susdits Conseils, toutes les lettres reçues, et le sujet de la réponse convenue.

ARTICLE XIV.

Le Grand Secrétaire écrira en marge des pétitions, lettres ou mémoires qui seront lus en Conseil, le sujet de la réponse convenue, et après en avoir rédigé les réponses, il les fera signer par le Grand Inspecteur Général ou son Député, par le Secrétaire de la juridiction, et le Grand Garde des Sceaux. Il les signera, scellera et les adressera lui-même.

Cependant, comme ce travail ne peut pas être fait pendant la séance du Conseil, et qu'il peut être quelquefois dangereux de retarder lesdites lettres, jusqu'au prochain Conseil, il produira la minute de la réponse pour qu'elle puisse être lue dans le prochain Conseil, et remettra tout ce qui y est relatif au Garde des Archives, pour que le Souverain Grand Conseil puisse y faire les corrections qu'il pensera convenable.

ARTICLE XV.

Les Conseils Particuliers, soit dans les villes de Paris ou Bordeaux, Provinces ou telles autres, n'auront pas le pouvoir d'envoyer des Constitutions ou Règlemens, à moins qu'ils n'y soient autorisés * par le Souverain Grand Conseil, le Grand Inspecteur ou son Député.

ARTICLE XVI.

Le Grand Garde des Sceaux et Timbres ne pourra sceller ni timbrer aucunes lettres, qu'elles n'aient avant été signées par le Se-

* À moins qu'ils ne soient autorisés, timbrés et scellés, &c.—*Aveilhé's* copy and *Recueil des Actes.*

established under the government of our Inspectors, or that of the Council of the Sublime Princes, the titles of their Lodges, the dates of their charters, and a statement of the titles, degrees, offices, dignities, civil conditions and places of residence of the members, conformably to those furnished by our Inspectors or their Deputies.

The day for the reception of the President in the particular Councils shall be fixed in the Grand Councils of Communication.

ARTICLE XIII.

The Grand Secretary shall also keep a record containing all the decisions and regulations of the Grand Council of Quarterly Communication, in which shall be stated all the matters determined in such Council, all the letters received, and the substance of the answer determined on, to each.

ARTICLE XIV,

The Grand Secretary shall endorse on the margin of all petitions, letters and memoirs read to the Council, the substance of the answer agreed on, which answer shall, when written, be signed by the Grand Inspector General or his Deputy, by the Secretary of the proper jurisdiction, and by the Grand Keeper of the Seals; and then the Grand Secretary shall himself sign, stamp and seal it, and transmit the answer.

But, as it may not be practicable to do this while the Council is in session, and as it might sometimes be dangerous to delay answering until the next Council, he shall produce the minute of the answer, that it may be read in the next Council, and shall deliver all that relates thereto to the Keeper of the Archives, that the Sovereign Grand Council may therein make such corrections as to it may seem proper.

ARTICLE XV.

The particular Councils, whether in the cities of Paris and Bordeux, in the Provinces or elsewhere, shall have no power to issue Charters or Regulations, unless they be authorized by the Sovereign Grand Council, the Grand Inspector, or his Deputy.

ARTICLE XVI,

The Grand Keeper of the Seals and Stamps shall stamp and seal no letter which has not first been signed by the Secretary-General,

erétaire Général, et par deux Secrétaires de différentes juridictions ;
ni ne peut timbrer ni sceller aucuns règlemens, avant qu'ils n'aient
été signés par le Grand Inspecteur ou son Député et par les susdits
trois Secrétaires, ni timbrer et sceller aucunes constitutions, à moins
qu'elles n'aient été signées par les susdits trois Grands Officiers et
autres Princes au nombre de sept, au moins, membres du Souverain
Grand Conseil des Princes Sublimes.

ARTICLE XVII.

Le Grand Trésorier doit être connu pour avoir une fortune aisée. Il
sera chargé de tous les fonds qui seront perçus pour l'entretien du
Souverain Grand Conseil, ou donnés par forme de charité. Il sera tenu
un régistre très exact de toutes les recettes, dépenses et charités, établies distinctement et de la manière dont les fonds ont été dépen-
sés. Ceux pour l'usage du Souverain Grand Conseil, et ceux des-
tinés pour les charités seront tenus séparément. Il sera donné un
reçu pour chaque somme, qui spécifiera le numéro du folio de son
régistre, et il ne sera payé aucune somme que par l'ordre écrit du
Président et des deux Grands Officiers du Souverain Grand
Conseil.

ARTICLE XVIII.

A la première Assemblée du Grand Conseil, qui suivra le 27 décembre, le Grand Trésorier rendra ses comptes.

ARTICLE XIX.

Nul ordre de recette, sur le Trésorier, ne sera délivré que par le
Président ou les deux Grands Surveillants, mais d'après une résolu-
tion du Grand Conseil, qui sera mentionnée dans ledit ordre, ainsi
que tous les paiements desdits fonds, auxquels il ne sera jamais
touché pour aucun banquet, lesquels seront payés à frais communs
par tous les F∴ F∴

ARTICLE XX.

Si aucuns mémoires, pétitions et plaintes étoient portés devant le
Souverain Grand Conseil, par un Conseil particulier, dont le Président seroit membre, il ne pourroit donner sa voix ni même son
avis, à moins qu'il en fût requis par le Président du Grand Conseil.

and by two Secretaries of different jurisdictions; nor can he stamp or seal any regulations that have not been signed by the Grand Inspector or his Deputy, and by said three Secretaries; and he can neither stamp or seal any Charter of Constitution that has not first been signed by the said three Grand Officers and by other Princes, to the number, in all, of seven at least, members of the Sovereign Grand Council of the Sublime Princes.

ARTICLE XVII.

The Grand Treasurer must be known to be a person of easy fortune. He shall have charge of all the funds received on account of the Sovereign Grand Council, or given by way of charity. An exact record shall be kept of all receipts, expenditures and charities, carefully distinguishing each, and showing how the moneys in each case have been expended; the funds of the Sovereign Grand Council, and those for charitable purposes, being always kept separate. A receipt shall be given for every sum, that shall refer to the number of the page of the register on which it is entered; and no moneys shall be paid out except on the written order of the President and of the two Grand Officers of the Sovereign Grand Council.

ARTICLE XVIII.

At the first Assembly of the Grand Council after the 27th of December, the Grand Treasurer shall lay before it his accounts.

ARTICLE XIX.

No order on the Treasurer for money shall be given except by the President or the two Grand Wardens; and that only on a resolution of the Grand Council, mentioned in the order, as also all payments of the said funds. None of the funds shall ever be used to pay for banquets, which shall always be paid for by common contributions of all the Brethren.

ARTICLE XX.

When any memoir, petition, or complaint is sent to the Sovereign Grand Council, by a particular Council, the President whereof is a member, he cannot vote, nor even express his opinion, unless requested to do so by the President of the Grand Council.

ARTICLE XXI.

Les Grands Inspecteurs Députés, et les deux premiers Grands Officiers ne peuvent être destitués par le Grand Conseil de Communication de quartier des Princes du Royal Secret, que pour de légitimes raisons mises en délibération, lorsqu'il y aura des preuves contre eux parfaitement démontrées ; mais les susdits Grands Officiers pourront donner leur démission dans le Grand Conseil. Les Grands Inspecteurs et Députés ne peuvent être remplaeés que par la nomination du Souverain des Souverains et des Très Puissants Princes du Grand Conseil de Communication.

ARTICLE XXII.

Le Grand Conseil visitera les Conseils particuliers, ainsi que les Loges de Perfection par les Députés Inspecteurs, ou en leur place par ceux qui seront nommés à cet effet, qui rendront compte de tout ce qui s'y sera passé, par écrit, au Secrétaire Général, afin d'en instruire le Grand Conseil. Ledit Grand Inspecteur ou Député visitera leurs travaux, les régistres, les Constitutions et les tableaux dudit Conseil ou des Loges de Perfection, et en dressera procès-verbal, qui sera signé par les Officiers-Dignitaires dudit Conseil ou Loges de Perfection, ou autres quelconques ; qu'il communiquera au Souverain Grand Conseil le plustôt possible, en l'adressant au Grand Secrétaire Général. Il présidera dans les susdits Grands Conseils ou Loges de Perfection, ou autres, toutes les fois qu'il en jugera nécessaire, sans opposition d'aucun frère, sous les peines de désobéissance et d'interdiction : car tel est notre bon plaisir.

ARTICLE XXIII.

Lorsque le Grand Conseil sera régulièrement convoqué, sept membres suffiront pour ouvrir les travaux, à l'heure indiquée; et les règlemens qui seront faits et passés à la pluralité des voix parmi eux auront force de loix, comme si les autres membres eussent été présents ; excepté dans les cas de nécessité, ou le Grand Inspecteur ou son Député peut procéder aux travaux avec trois membres.

ARTICLE XXIV.

Si dans l'assemblée d'un Grand Conseil aucun membre se présentoit d'une manière indécente, pris de vin, ou commettroit quel-

ARTICLE XXI.

The Grand Inspectors and Deputies, and the two first Grand Officers can be removed from office only by the Grand Council of Quarterly Communication of the Princes of the Royal Secret, for legitimate reasons openly discussed, and when the proofs against them are clear and conclusive; but these officers may resign in the Grand Council. The Grand Inspectors and Deputies can be replaced only by appointment by the Sovereign of the Sovereigns and the Most Puissant Princes of the Grand Quarterly Council.

ARTICLE XXII.

The Grand Council will visit the particular Councils and Lodges of Perfection through their Deputies Inspectors, or, in their place, through persons specially appointed therefor; who shall report in writing to the Secretary General all that occurs on their visitation, that the Sovereign Grand Council may be informed thereof. The Grand Inspector or Deputy shall inspect the work, the registers, charters and lists of members of such Councils and Lodges of Perfection, and shall draw up a statement thereof, which shall be signed by the Officers-Dignitaries of said Councils or Lodges of Perfection, or other bodies, and which he shall forward to the Sovereign Grand Council as soon as possible, addressed to the Grand Secretary General.

He shall preside in said Grand Councils, Lodges of Perfection, and other bodies, whenever he sees fit, without objection on the part of any brother whatever, under the penalties due to disobedience, and that of interdiction, for such is our good pleasure.

ARTICLE XXIII.

When the Grand Council shall be regularly convoked, seven members shall suffice to open the works at the time fixed; and the regulations then made and passed by a plurality of votes, shall have the force of law, as if the other members had been present; except in cases of emergency, when the Grand Inspector or his Deputy, with three members, may proceed with the work.

ARTICLE XXIV.

If in a meeting of a Grand Council any member should present himself in an indecent manner, intoxicated, or doing any other act

ques fautes, tendantes à détruire l'harmonie qui doit régner dans
ces respectables assemblées, il sera réprimandé pour la première
fois ; à la seconde offense, mis à l'amende fixée à la majorité, qui
sera immédiatement payée, et pour la troisième fois, il sera privé
de ses dignités, et si la majorité du Grand Conseil est pour l'ex-
pulsion, il sera chassé.

ARTICLE XXV.

Si dans le Souverain Grand Conseil, aucun membre étoit coupa-
ble de quelques offences mentionnées dans le précédent article, il
sera pour la première fois condamné à telle amende, qui lui sera
immédiatement imposée ; pour la seconde fois, il sera chassé de
l'Assemblée Générale, l'espace d'une année, pendant lequel temps
il sera privé de ses fonctions dans le Conseil ou dans la Loge dont
il seroit membre ; et pour la troisième fois, il sera chassé pour toujours. S'il est Président de quelque Conseil ou Loge particulière,
il en sera déchu ; il sera nommé un nouveau Président à son Conseil ou Loge, de quelque grade que ce soit.

ARTICLE XXVI.

Le Souverain Grand Conseil ne réconnoîtra pour Conseils régu-
liers ou Loges de Perfection que ceux qui seront régulièrement
constitués par lui ou par les Grands Inspecteurs ou leurs Députés ;
et il en sera de même à l'égard des Chevaliers Maçons, Princes et
Grands Elus Parfaits qui auroient été reçus par quelques Conseils
ou Loges qui n'y auroient pas été duement autorisés.

ARTICLE XXVII.

Toutes petitions au Souverain Grand Conseil pour obtenir des
lettres de Constitution, soit pour établir ou pour régler un Conseil
ou Loge quelconque, seront envoyées, savoir : pour la Province, aux
Inspecteurs de la même juridiction, qui nommeront quatre Commissaires à cet effet, pour prendre toutes les informations nécessaires ; à cet effet, ils enverront aux Inspecteurs ou leur Député
dans ladite juridiction, une liste exacte des membres qui de-
mandent la création d'un Conseil ou Loge de Perfection, etc.,
pour, sur le rapport desdits Commissaires et celui du Grand Inspecteur ou son Député, être déterminé par le Grand Conseil sur la de-
mande desdits membres. Quand ce sera pour les Pays Etrangers,

that may tend to interrupt the harmony that ought to reign in a body so respectable, he shall, for the first offence, be reprimanded ; for the second a fine shall be imposed, fixed by the voice of the majority, to be paid forthwith ; and for the third, he shall be deprived of his dignities, and if a majority of the Grand Council so decide, he shall be expelled.

ARTICLE XXV.

If in the Sovereign Grand Council any member be guilty of any of the offences mentioned in the preceding article, he shall, for the first offence, be condemned to pay such fine as may be forthwith imposed on him; for the second, he shall be excluded from the General Assembly for the space of one year, during which time he shall be deprived of his functions in the Council and in the Lodge whereof he is a member ; and for the third he shall be expelled. If he be the President of a particular Council or Lodge, he will be deprived of his office, which will be filled by a new appointment, whatever may be the degree of his Council or Lodge.

☐ ARTICLE XXVI.

The Sovereign Grand Council will recognize as regular no other Councils or Lodges of Perfection than those regularly constituted by itself or by the Grand Inspectors or their Deputies; nor any Knights Masons, Princes, or Perfect Grand Elus, that have been made such by any Council or Lodge not duly authorized.

ARTICLE XXVII.

All petitions addressed to the Sovereign Grand Council for charters, or for the establishment or regularization of any Council or Lodge, shall be referred as follows : if from a Province, to the Inspectors for that jurisdiction, who shall thereupon appoint four Commissioners, to obtain all the necessary information, to which end they shall furnish to the Inspectors or their Deputy for that jurisdiction, an exact list of the members who apply for the establishment of such Council or Lodge of Perfection, &c.; to the end that, upon the report of such Commissioners, or upon that of the Grand Inspector, or his Deputy, the Grand Council may decide upon the application. If from a foreign country, the proper Grand Inspectors may, each

les Grand Inspecteurs, dans leurs juridictions, pourront créer, constituer, défendre, révoquer et exclure, selon leur prudence, de quoi
ils dresseront procès-verbal, et donneront avis de tout ce qu'ils auront fait au Souverain Grand Conseil, par l'occasion la plus favorable. Les susdits Inspecteurs se conformeront aux loix et coutumes ainsi qu'aux Constitutions secrètes du Souverain Grand Conseil. Ils auront la liberté de choisir les Députés dans leurs travaux
pour accélérer, et de les autoriser par lettres patentes qui auront
force et validité.

ARTICLE XXVIII.

Le Souverain Grand Conseil n'accordera aucune constitution
pour l'établissement d'une Loge Royale de Perfection, excepté aux
Frères qui auront au moins le grade de Prince de Jérusalem ; et
pour l'établissement d'un Conseil de Chevaliers d'Orient, celui de
Chevalier d'Orient et d'Occident ; mais pour l'établissement d'un
Conseil de Prince de Jérusalem, le Frère doit avoir absolument le
grade de Sublime Chevalier, Prince Adepte, et prouver par ses
titres authentiques qu'il a légitimement et régulièrement été reçu,
et prouver qu'il a toujours joui librement d'un bien honnête, libre
de reproches par une bonne réputation et une bonne conduite, et
qu'il a en tous temps été soumis aux décrets du Souverain Grand
Conseil des Princes dont il désire devenir le Chef.

ARTICLE XXIX.

Le Souverain Conseil des Princes Sublimes n'accordera aucunes
nouvelles Patentes ni Constitutions, soit pour Paris ou Bordeaux,
Provinces ou Pays Etrangers, qu'en fournissant un reçu du Grand
Trésorier, de la somme de vingt-quatre shellings pour le paiement
des personnes employées à cet ouvrage. Les Grands Inspecteurs
des Orients Etrangers s'y conformeront dans les mêmes cas ; suivant
les voyages qu'ils seront obligés de faire, défrayés de toutes dépenses. En outre, ils ne délivreront ni Commission ni pouvoir à
aucun Prince Maçon, avant d'avoir signé sa soumission dans les
régistres du Grand Secrétaire Général, du Grand Inspecteur ou
son Député, et pour les Provinces et Pays Etrangers dans ceux de
nos Inspecteurs ou Députés. Il est même nécessaire que la susdite
soumission soit écrite et signée par ledit Frère.

within his jurisdiction, create, constitute, prohibit, revoke and exclude, according as their judgment may direct, sending up full report of their action in the premises to the Sovereign Grand Council by the first favorable opportunity. And the said Inspectors shall conform to the laws and customs, as also to the Secret Constitutions of the Sovereign Grand Council. They may, for greater despatch, appoint Deputies to act for them, empowering them by letters patent that shall have force and validity.

ARTICLE XXVIII.

The Sovereign Grand Council will grant charters to establish a Royal Lodge of Perfection to no brothers who have not attained, at least, to the degree of Princes of Jerusalem ; and to establish a Council of Knights of the East, to no one who has not attained that of Knights of the East and West. To obtain authority to establish a Council of Princes of Jerusalem, the brother must necessarily have the degree of Sublime Knight Prince Adept, and must prove by authentic documents that he has been legitimately and regularly received as such ; and he must show that he has always led an honest life, free of any reproach, and been distinguished by a good reputation and an upright course of conduct ; and also that he has ever been obedient to the decrees of the Sovereign Grand Council of the Princes, among whom he desires to be a chief.

ARTICLE XXIX.

The Sovereign Council of the Sublime Princes will grant no new Patents or Constitutions, whether for Paris or Bordeaux, for a Province or for foreign countries, unless upon the production of a receipt of the Grand Treasurer for the sum of twenty-four shillings, to pay the persons employed in that labour. The Grand Inspectors of Foreign Orients will observe the same rule in like cases. All the expenses of any journeys which they are obliged to make are to be defrayed. Moreover, they will deliver neither commission nor power to any Prince Mason until he has first signed his submission in the register of the Grand Secretary General, of the Grand Inspector or his Deputy ; and, in a Province or a foreign country, in those of our Inspectors or Deputies. It is even necessary that such submission be both written and signed by such brother.

ARTICLE XXX.

Si les Inspecteurs ou Députés jugeroient convenable de visiter dans quelques lieux des deux hémisphères, soit le Grand Conseil des Princes de Jérusalem ou quelqu'autre, ils se présenteront * avec les décorations de leurs dignités, soit à la porte du Grand Conseil des Princes de Jérusalem, Grand Chapitre des Chevaliers de l'Aigle Noir, ou Consistoire des Princes Adeptes, ou enfin à telle autre que ce soit, ils seront reçus avec tous les honneurs qui leur sont dus, et jouiront en tous lieux de leurs priviléges et prérogatives, etc., etc. L'inspecteur ou son Député, ainsi que les Chevaliers, Princes Maçons, lorsqu'ils visiteront une Loge de Royale Perfection, ou aucune autre quelconque, le Puissant Grand-Maître, le Respectable d'une Loge Symbolique enverra cinq officiers-dignitaires pour introduire le Prince Inspecteur ou son Député avec tous les honneurs tels qu'ils seront ci-après expliqués.

ARTICLE XXXI.

Les Princes de Jérusalem étant les Vaillants Princes de la Maçonnerie renouvelée, seront reçus avec les honneurs et jouiront de tous leurs priviléges dans toutes les Loges et Chapitres, ainsi que dans les Conseils de Chevaliers d'Orient, où ils feront leur entrée triomphante de la manière suivante :

1er. Les Princes de Jérusalem ont le droit d'annuler et révoquer ce qui peut avoir été fait en Conseil de Chevalier d'Orient, ainsi que dans les Loges de Royale Perfection et d'aucune autre de quelque grade que ce puisse être, quand ils ne seront pas conformes aux jugements et aux loix de l'ordre, pourvu néanmoins qu'il ne soit présent aucun Sublime Prince d'un Grade Supérieur.

2e. Quand un Prince de Jérusalem est annoncé à la porte d'une Loge Royale ou Chapitre, ou aucune autre, avec les titres et ornements qui le font connoître comme tel, ou est connu par quelque Prince du même grade, le Respectable ou le Très Puissant d'une telle Loge enverra quatre Frères, Officiers dignitaires, pour l'introduire et l'accompagner. Il entrera le chapeau sur la tête, ou son casque, l'épée nue à la main droite, comme un combattant, le bouclier au bras gauche, et même cuirassé, s'il est absolument décoré de

---

* " Ou aucuns autres quelconques, lorsqu'ils seront connus et munis de titres authentiques, se présenteront."—*Aveilhé's copy.*

ARTICLE XXX.

If the Inspectors or Deputies see fit to visit anywhere in the two hemispheres a Grand Council of Princes of Jerusalem, a Council of Knights of the East, a Lodge of Perfection, or any other body whatsoever, they will present themselves,* clothed with the decorations of their rank, at the door of the Grand Council of Princes of Jerusalem, of the Grand Chapter of the Knights of the Black Eagle, or of the Consistory of the Princes Adepts, or of any other body, as the case may be, and will be there received with all the honours due them, and everywhere enjoy their privileges and prerogatives. Whenever an Inspector or his Deputy, or any other Knight Prince Mason visits a Lodge of Royal Perfection, or other Lodge, the Puissant Grand Master or the Venerable Master of a Symbolic Lodge will send out five officers-dignitaries to introduce the Prince Inspector or his Deputy, with all the honours hereinafter prescribed and explained.

ARTICLE XXXI.

The Princes of Jerusalem being the Valiant Princes of the Renovated Masonry, they will be received with all the honours, and will enjoy all their privileges, in all Lodges and Chapters, as well as in all Councils of Knights of the East, whereinto they will make their triumphant entry in the following manner:

1st. The Princes of Jerusalem have the right to annul and revoke whatever may have been transacted in a Council of Knights of the East, in Lodges of Royal Perfection, or in other Lodges of whatever degree, wherein such bodies have not conformed to the decisions and laws of the order; *provided, however,* that there be present no Sublime Prince of a higher degree.

2d. When a Prince of Jerusalem is announced, as such, at the door of a Royal Lodge or of a Chapter, or of any other Lodge, with the evidences and ornaments that prove him to be such, or when he is known to be such by some Prince of the same degree, the Venerable, or the Th∴ Puissant Grand Master, will send four officers-dignitaries to introduce and accompany him.

He will enter, wearing his hat or helmet, his drawn sword in his right hand, as one in a combat, buckler on his left arm, and even cuirassed, if fully clothed with all his insignia and ornaments.

---

* " Or any other body whatsoever, when they are recognized, and furnished with authentic evidence of their rank, they will present themselves."—*Aveilhé's copy.*

tous ses attributs et ornements. Le Prince visiteur étant à l'Occident, entre les deux Surveillants, accompagné des quatre Députés de la Loge, saluera : 1o. le Maître, 2o. au Nord et au Sud, 3o. le 1er. et le 2d. Surveillants. Aussitôt après cette cérémonie, il fera le signe du grade que l'on tient, qui sera répété par le Maître et par tous les F.·. F.·. ensemble ; et ensuite [le Vénérable] dira, "*A l'Ordre, mes Frères !*" A l'instant, tous les Frères du Nord et du Sud formeront ensemble une voute avec leurs épées nues, et à ce défaut, avec leurs bras tendus, sous laquelle le Valeureux Prince passera d'un pas grave, jusqu'à ce qu'il soit arrivé au Maître. Le Maître lui offrira le sceptre qu'il acceptera et commandera les travaux : le Maître lui rendra compte des travaux et de tout ce qui a rapport à l'Ordre, ou, s'il juge à propos, il laissera le sceptre au Maître pour continuer les travaux déjà commencés ; et si le Valeureux Prince veut se retirer avant la clôture de la Loge, après en avoir informé le Respectable ou Très Puissant qui le remerciera de sa visite, l'insistera à la faire souvent, et lui offrira tous ses services, après ce compliment, il frappera un grand coup et dira : "*A l'Ordre, mes Frères !*" ce qui sera répété par les Surveillants, et tous les F.·. F.·. du Nord et du Sud formeront une voute sous laquelle le Valeureux Prince, après avoir salué le Maître, passera, l'épée nue, comme un combattant. Arrivé entre les deux Surveillants, il se retournera vers l'Orient, saluera le Maître, au Nord et au Midi, et ensuite les deux Surveillants ; [et] toujours accompagné des quatre Députés, il sortira de la Loge, dont les portes seront toutes grandes ouvertes, comme quand il est entré. Les quatre Députés étant rentrés, les travaux seront continués.

3e. Tous les Princes de Jérusalem ne peuvent jouir de leurs priviléges, quand il y a un Prince Adepte, Chevalier Noachite, ou un Souverain Prince du Royal Secret présent ; mais ils peuvent faire leur entrée avec tous les honneurs, si les Princes Sublimes présents y consentent.

4e. Les Princes de Jérusalem seront nommés en Loge, *Valeureux Princes ;* le Chevalier Adepte, *de Souverain Prince ;* et les Chevaliers du Royal Secret, *Illustres Souverains des Souverains Princes Sublimes ;* les Chevaliers d'Orient, *Excellents F.·. F.·. Chevaliers.* Le Chevalier d'Orient aura le droit, quand un Prince de Jérusalem ne sera pas présent, de demander compte exact de tout ce qui s'est passé en Loge, de voir si leurs Constitutions sont

When the Prince Visitor, thus entering, is in the West, between the Wardens, and accompanied by the four deputies of the Lodge, he will salute, first the Master, then the North, then the South, and then the two Wardens. Immediately after this ceremony he will give the sign of the degree in which the body is working, which will be repeated by the Master and by all the Brethren together; and then the Master will say, " *To order, my Brethren!* " Instantly all the Brethren on the North and South will together form an arch with their naked swords, or if they have none, with their outstretched arms, under which the Valorous Prince will pass with a grave step until he comes to the Master. The Master will offer him the sceptre, which he will accept and direct the work. The Master will report to him in regard to the work, and as to every thing that concerns the order. But if he thinks proper, he will decline to receive the sceptre, leaving the Master to continue the work already begun; and if the Valorous Prince desires to retire before the Lodge is closed, he will so inform the Master or Th∴ Puissant, who will thank him for his visit, invite him to frequently repeat it, and tender him all the services in his power; and after this compliment, the Master will give one rap, and say, " *To order, my Brethren!* " This will be repeated by each Warden, and all the Brethren on the North and South will form a vault, under which the Valorous Prince, after saluting the Master, will pass, his naked sword in his hand, as if in a combat. When between the two Wardens, he will turn towards the East and salute the Master, the North, the South, and each Warden, in succession. Then, still accompanied by the four Deputies, he will retire from the Lodge, the doors standing wide open as when he entered. The four Deputies having reëntered, the work will be resumed.

3d. A Prince of Jerusalem cannot exercise his privileges when there is also present a Prince Adept, Chevalier Noachite, or Sovereign Prince of the Royal Secret; but he may enter with all the honours if the Sublime Princes present assent thereto.

4th. When present in a Lodge, Princes of Jerusalem will be addressed as *Valiant Princes;* Knights Adept as *Sovereign Princes;* Knights of the Royal Secret as *Illustrious Sovereigns of the Sovereign Sublime Princes;* and Knights of the East as *Excellent Brother-Knights.* A Knight of the East will have the right, when a Prince of Jerusalem is not present, to require a full account of whatever work has been done in the Lodge; to see if its Consti-

bonnes et en forme, et de mettre la paix entre les F.˙.F.˙. s'il existoit quelques froideurs ou contestations entr'eux ; d'exclure le plus obstiné et ceux qui ne se soumettroient pas d'eux-mêmes aux statuts et loix qui leur sont prescrits par nos Secrètes Constitutions et autres, soit en Loge de Perfection ou Symbolique.

5e. Les Valeureux Princes de Jérusalem ont le droit, ainsi que les Chevaliers d'Orient, de s'asseoir le chapeau sur la tête pendant les travaux des Loges de Perfection et Symboliques, s'ils le veulent. Néanmoins ils ne peuvent jouir de leurs priviléges que quand ils sont regulièrement connus et décorés des ornements et attributs de leur dignité.

6e. Cinq Valeureux Princes de Jérusalem pourront former un Conseil de Chevaliers d'Orient partout où il n'y en aura pas d'établi. Ils seront juges ; mais obligés de donner avis de leurs travaux au Souverain Grand Conseil, ainsi qu'au plus près Inspecteur ou son Député par écrit. Ils y sont autorisés par les pouvoirs qui en ont été donnés à leurs Illustres Prédecesseurs par le peuple de Jérusalem, à leur retour d'ambassade à Babylone.

ARTICLE XXXII.

Pour établir entre tous les Conseils particuliers, et parmi tous les illustres Chevaliers et Princes Maçons une Correspondance régulière, ils enverront chaque année au Souverain Grand Conseil, et à chaque [Grand] Conseil particulier, un état général de tous les Conseils particuliers régulièrement établis, ainsi que les noms des Officiers du Souverain Grand Conseil des Sublimes Princes ; et donneront avis, dans le cours de l'année, de tous les changements intéressants qui pourroient avoir eu lieu depuis leur dernier état.*

ARTICLE XXXIII.

Pour maintenir l'ordre et la discipline, le Souverain Grand Conseil des Princes Sublimes du Royal Secret ne s'assemblera pour procéder à aucun travail Maçonnique qu'une fois par an ; alors personne ne sera admis au Sublime et dernier Grade de la Maçonnerie que les trois plus anciens Chevaliers Adeptes, qui seront proclamés à la Grande Loge du Grand Elu Parfait Maître, soit en Conseil, Chapitre, &c.

* Cet article est entièrement corrompu, et il doit, je crois, se lire comme suit : " Pour établir, &c., ils enverront chaque année au Souverain Gd. Conseil, à chaque Grand Conseil, et à tous les Conseils particuliers régulièrement établis, un état général de tous leurs membres, ainsi que les noms de leurs Officiers ; et donneront avis au Souverain Gd. Conseil des Sublimes Princes, dans le cours de l'année, &c."

tutions (charter) are valid and in form; to reconcile matters among the brethren, if there be coldness or contention among them, and to exclude any one who obstinately refuses to submit, and any who will not of their own accord pay obedience to the Statutes and to the Laws contained in our Secret Constitutions and others, whether in a Lodge of Perfection or a Symbolic Lodge.

5th. The Valorous Princes of Jerusalem and the Knights of the East are entitled to sit covered during the labours of a Lodge of Perfection or Symbolic Lodge, but they enjoy their privileges only when legally known, and when clothed with the ornaments and insignia of their rank.

6th. Five Valiant Princes of Jerusalem may form a Council of Knights of the East, wherever none has been established. They will be invested with judicial power, but must give an account of their work to the Sovereign Grand Council, and to the nearest Grand Inspector or his Deputy, in writing. Their authority as Judges is derived from the powers given their illustrious predecessors by the people of Jerusalem, on their return from their embassy to Babylon.

ARTICLE XXXII.

To establish among all the Subordinate Councils, and among all the Illustrious Knights and Princes Masons, a regular system of correspondence, they will send up every year to the Sovereign Grand Council, and to each particular Council, a general statement of all the particular Councils regularly constituted, and of the names of the officers of the Sovereign Grand Council of the Sublime Princes, and will give information, during the year, of any changes of importance since the last statement.*

ARTICLE XXXIII.

To maintain order and discipline, the Sovereign Grand Council of the Sublime Princes of the Royal Secret will meet but once a year, to proceed in their masonic labours. At such meeting there will be admitted to the Sublime and last degree of Masonry no more than three of the oldest Knights Adepts, who will be proclaimed in the Grand Lodge of Perfect Grand Elect Masters, or in Council, Chapter, &c.

* This article is evidently corrupted, and ought, I imagine, to read, "To establish, &c.; they will send every year to the Sov.·. Gr.·. Council, to each Gr.·. Council, and to all the particular Councils regularly established, a general statement of all their members, and the names of their officers, and will report to the Sov.·. Gr.·. Council, during the course of the year, all changes of importance since the last statement."

ARTICLE XXXIV.

Jours de Fetes *que les Chevaliers Princes Maçons et Valeureux Princes de Jérusalem sont tenus de célébrer particulièrement :*

1o. Le 20 Novembre ; jour mémorable, où leurs ancêtres firent leur entrée à Jérusalem.

2o. Le 23 Février, pour louer le Seigneur à l'occasion de la reconstruction du Temple,

3o. Les Chevaliers d'Orient célèbrent le Saint Jour de la ré-édification du Temple de Dieu, le 22 Mars et le 22 Septembre, jours d'équinoxes ou renouvellement des jours longs et courts, en mémoire de ce que le Temple fut bâti deux fois. Tous les Princes Maçons sont obligés d'aller au conseil d'Orient, pour célébrer ces deux jours ; et les travaux n'en seront ouverts qu'avec les cérémonies d'usage.

4o. Le Grand Elu Parfait célébrera aussi en outre et en particulier la dédicace du premier Temple, le 5e jour de la 3e Lune, qui répond à notre mois de Juillet, où les Chevaliers et Princes Maçons seront décorés de tous leurs ornements.

ARTICLE XXXV.

Un Conseil particulier des Princes du Royal Secret ne pourra excéder le nombre de 15, y compris les Officiers.

Chaque année, le jour de St. Jean l'Evangéliste,* chaque Grand Conseil particulier doit nommer neuf Officiers, non compris le Président qui doit être toujours continué trois ans.

1o. Le Lieutenant-Commandant, qui préside en l'absence du Souverain Grand Commandant.

2o. Le Grand Surveillant, qui préside en l'absence des deux premiers.

3o. Le Grand Garde des Sceaux ou Grand Secrétaire.

4o. Le Grand Trésorier.

5o. Le Grand Capitaine des Gardes,

6o. Le Grand Introducteur.

7o. Le Grand Maître Architecte ou Ingénieur.

8o. Le Grand Hospitalier.

9o. Le Grand Orateur ou Ministre d'État (qui doit être le 6e),†

---

* ' Baptiste ' : *Aveilhé's* copy.

† J'ai faite cette correction dans la traduction,

ARTICLE XXXIV.

FEAST-DAYS, *which the Knights Princes-Masons and Valorous Princes of Jerusalem are bound specially to celebrate.*

1st. The 20th of November, the memorable day when their ancestors made their entry into Jerusalem.

2d. The 23d of February, to praise the Lord on account of the rebuilding of the Temple.

3d. The Knights of the East will celebrate the Holy Day of the rebuilding of the Temple of God, the 22d of March and the 22d of September, which are the equinoctial days, when the day and the night respectively begin to lengthen; in memory of the fact that the Temple was twice builded. All the Princes Masons are bound to attend the Council of the East to celebrate these two days; and that body must, on such occasion, be opened in due form.

4th. The Grand Elect Perfect [Masons] will also and in a special manner celebrate the dedication of the First Temple on the 5th day of the 3d month, which answers to our month of July; on which occasion the Knights and Princes Masons are to wear all their decorations.

ARTICLE XXXV.

A particular Council of the Princes of the Royal Secret can consist of no more than fifteen members, the officers included.

Every year, on the day of St. John the Evangelist, every Grand Particular Council must elect nine officers, not including the President, who is always to serve three years.

1st. The LIEUTENANT-COMMANDANT, who presides in the absence of the Sovereign Grand Commandant.

2d. The GRAND WARDEN, who presides in the absence of the two former.

3d. The GRAND KEEPER OF THE SEALS, or GRAND SECRETARY.

4th. The GRAND TREASURER.

5th. The GRAND CAPTAIN OF THE GUARDS.

6th. The GRAND ORATOR, or MINISTER OF STATE.

7th. The GRAND USHER.

8th. The GRAND MASTER ARCHITECT, or ENGINEER.

9th. The GRAND HOSPITALLER.

Tous les autres réunis sous les ordres du Souverain des Souverains Princes et [ou?] son Lieutenant-Commandant, restent sans changement, et il ne peut en être admis aucun autre au-delà du nombre 15.

Ce Grand Conseil est sujet au Grand Inspecteur ou son Député, comme Chef, et reconnu comme tel dans toutes les occasions, et sous l'obéissance de leur Conseil, pour ce qui concerne l'Art Royal, ainsi que dans les Grades inférieurs.

Nous, Souverains des Souverains Princes Sublimes du Royal Secret de l'Ordre Royal et Militaire de la plus Respectable Fraternité des Libres et Acceptés Maçons, avons délibérés et résolus que ces présents Statuts, Règlemens et Constitutions seront observés.

Ordonnons à nos Grands Inspecteurs et leurs Députés de faire lire et recevoir, soit dans tous les Conseils particuliers, Chapitres et Loges Royales et dans aucune autre quelconque.

*Au Grand Orient de Bordeaux, sous la Céleste Voûte, les jours et ans susdites.

Certifié sincère et véritable, conforme à la remise qui en a été faite par l'Illustre F∴ Hyman Isaac Long, aux Archives du Grand

---

* La conclusion et attestation dans la copie d'Aveilhé sont comme suit :

" Au Grand Orient de Paris et Bordeaux sous la Voûte Céleste, les jours et an susdites.

Nous soussignés, Députés Inspecteurs Généraux et Princes Maçons, etc., etc., etc., certifions que les Règlemens et Constitutions transcrites des autres parts et donnés par la Grande Loge et Souverain Grand Conseil des Sublimes Princes de la Maçonnerie, au Grand Orient de France, au très puissant et respectable frère Etienne Morin sont conformes à l'original, dont il a transmis copie au très respectable frère Frankin, Député Grand Inspecteur en l'Isle de la Jamaïque, et encore conformes à la copie dûment en forme qu'on a rémis dans les Archives de la Loge Sublime, à l'Orient de Charleston le très respectable frère Hyman Isaac Long, lorsqu'il a constituée ; et que foy doit y être ajoutée.

A l'Orient de Charleston, Caroline du Sud, le 9me jour du 4me mois appellé Tammuz, de l'année 5557 de la Restauration et de l'ère Vulgaire le 9 juin 1797.

Signés... H. I. Long, Député Inspecteur Général Prince Maçon, etc., etc., etc.; Delahogue, Député Inspecteur Général Prince Maçon, etc., etc., etc. Auguste De Grasse, Député Inspecteur G'l. Prince Maçon, etc., etc., etc. Saint Paul, Député Grand Inspecteur P'ce Maçon, etc., etc., etc.; Robin, Député Grand Inspecteur P'ce. Maçon, etc., etc., etc., et Petit, Député Inspecteur G'l. Prince Maçon, etc. etc., etc.

Je Soussigné, Député Grand Inspecteur Général Prince Maçon, etc., etc., etc., certifie que les Règlemens et Constitutions cy dessus et des autres parts transcrits est conforme à la copie qui m'en a été transmise par les cy dessus soussignés ; et quelle est fidellement extraite de mon registre, et que foy doit y estre ajoutée.

Au Port-au-Prince, le 10eme jour du 10eme mois appellé Thebat de l'an 5557, de la Restauration, et de l'Ere Vulgaire le 10 Décembre 1797. Bte. Aveilhé, D. G. I. G. & M.

[Et à la marge] Vu par nous à Charleston, le 12 Mars 5802. Auguste de Grasse, K. H. P. R. S. Souverain Grand Inspecteur Général du 33me degré, Souverain Grand Commandeur pour les Isles Françaises de l'Amérique du vent et sous le vent.

All the other members, united under the orders of the Sovereign of the Sovereign Princes, or of his Lieutenant Commandant, remain without change; and no member can be admitted, if thereby the number will exceed fifteen in all.

This Grand Council is subject to the Grand Inspector or his Deputy, as its Chief, to be recognized as such on all occasions; and it is subordinate to the Council in whatever concerns the Royal Art, both in the high and the inferior degrees.

WE, Sovereign of the Sovereign Sublime Princes of the Royal Secret of the Royal and Military Order of the Most Worshipful Fraternity of Free and Accepted Masons, have determined, and do resolve, that these present Statutes, Regulations and Constitutions shall be observed.

And we do order our Grand Inspectors and their Deputies to cause them to be read and received, as well in all particular Councils, Chapters and Royal Lodges, as in all other bodies whatsoever.

* DONE at the Grand Orient of Bordeaux, under the Celestial Vault, the day and year above mentioned.

* The conclusion and attestation in *Aveilhé's* copy are as follows :

"DONE at the Grand Orient of Paris and Bordeaux, under the Celestial Vault, the day and year aforesaid.

"WE, the undersigned, Deputy Inspectors General and Princes Masons, &c., &c., &c., do certify that the Regulations and Constitutions above transcribed and furnished by the Grand Lodge and Sovereign Grand Council at the Grand Orient of France to the Th∴ P∴ and Resp∴ Bro∴ STEPHEN MORIN, agree with the original, whereof he delivered a copy to the Th∴ Resp∴ Bro∴ Franklin, Deputy Grand Inspector in the Island of Jamaica ; and that they also agree with the copy thereof in due form deposited in the archives of the Sublime Lodge at the Orient of Charleston by the Th∴ Resp∴ Bro∴ Hyman Isaac Long, when he constituted that body ; and that full faith and credit should be given thereto.

"ORIENT OF CHARLESTON, South Carolina, the 9th day of the 4th month called Tammuz, of the year 5557 of the Restoration, and of the Vulgar Era, 9th June, 1797.

"*Signed:* H. I. LONG, Deputy Inspector General, Prince Mason, &c., &c., &c.; DELAHOGUE, Deputy Inspector General, Prince Mason, &c., &c., &c.; AUGUSTE DE GRASSE, Deputy Inspector General, Prince Mason, &c., &c., &c.; SAINT PAUL, Deputy Grand Inspector, Prince Mason, &c., &c., &c.; ROBIN, Deputy Grand Inspector, Prince Mason, &c., &c., &c.; and PETIT, Deputy Grand Inspector, Prince Mason, &c., &c., &c.

"I, the undersigned, Deputy Grand Inspector General, Prince Mason, &c., &c., &c., do certify that the Regulations and Constitutions above and hereinbefore transcribed agree with the copy furnished by the above named ; that the same are faithfully copied from my register, and that full faith and credit ought to be given them.

"Port-au-Prince, the 10th day of the 10th month called Thebat, of the year of the Restoration 5557, and of the Vulgar Era the 10th December, 1797.
                                                    "B'TE AVEILHÉ,
                                                        D. G. I. G. and M.

[*And in the margin.*] "VISÉD by me at Charleston, the 12th of March, 5802. AUGUSTE DE GRASSE, K∴ H∴ P∴ R∴ S∴, Sov∴ Grand Inspector General, of the 33d Degree, Sov∴ Gr∴ Commander for the Windward and Leeward French Isles of America."

Conseil des Souverains Princes du Royal Secret à l'Orient de Charleston, Caroline du Sud, et certifié par luy et signé comme Député Grand Inspecteur Général et Prince Maçon.

J'<small>N</small> B'<small>TE</small> M'<small>IE</small> D<small>ELAHOGUE</small>,

Député G'd Insp. G'l P'e Maçon.

Souverain Grand Commandeur

du C'l. Sublime, Orient de Charleston, C'. du Sud.

A'<small>DRE</small>. F. A<small>UGUSTE</small> <small>DE</small> G<small>RASSE</small>,

Grand Garde des Sceaux et Archives.

Certified to be a true and correct copy, conformably to that deposited by the Ill.·. Bro.·. Hyman Isaac Long, in the archives of the Grand Council of the Sovereign Princes of the Royal Secret at the Orient of Charleston, South Carolina, and as certified and signed by him in his character of Deputy Grand Inspector General and Prince Mason.

JN. B'TE M'IE DELAHOGUE,
Dep'y Gr.·. Insp.·. Gen.·. Pr.·. M'n,
Sov.·. Gr.·. Commander of the Subl.·.
Council, O.·. of Charleston, South Carolina.

SEAL
OF THE
GR. COUNCIL.

A'DRE F. AUGUSTE DE GRASSE,
　　　　Grand Keeper of the Seals and Archives.

STATUTS ET REGLEMENS

POUR LE GOUVERNEMENT DE

TOUTES LES LOGES ROYALES REGULIERES DE PERFECTION

TRANSMIS PAR LE SOUVERAIN GRAND CONSEIL DES PRINCES SUBLIMES DU ROYAL SECRET,

à Berlin, Paris et Bordeaux.

ARTICLE I.

NULLES Loges de Grand Élu Parfait, Maître Sublime ne pour-roient procéder à aucuns travaux maçonniques, soit pour élection ou réception, à moins qu'elles ne soient munies de Constitutions des Princes Sublimes du Royal Secret ou Grand Inspecteur de l'Ordre ou son Député, dûment signées et scellées; à défaut de quoi elles seront réputées irrégulières, et ses travaux déclarés nuls.

ARTICLE II.

Aucune Loge de Grand Élu Parfait, Maître Sublime ne peut avoir correspondance avec aucune autre, excepté celles envoyées par le Secrétaire Général du Grand Conseil au Grand Inspecteur ou son Député, et communiquées par eux.

ARTICLE III.

Quand une Loge de Perfection connoîtra ou découvrira une Loge de Perfection qui ne sera pas comprise dans l'état délivré par le Grand Inspecteur ou son Député, elle doit en donner avis sur le champ au Grand Inspecteur ou son Député, pour qu'il en soit communiqué au Grand Conseil.

ARTICLE IV.

Si quelques frères s'assembloient irrégulièrement pour initier quelqu'uns à ce grade, ils doivent être réprimandés ; aucuns ma-çons d'une Loge régulière ne doivent les reconnoître ni les visiter sous telles peines prononcées par les loix des Loges de Perfection.

STATUTES AND REGULATIONS

FOR THE GOVERNMENT OF ALL

REGULAR LODGES OF PERFECTION,

TRANSMITTED BY THE

SOVEREIGN GRAND COUNCIL OF THE SUBLIME PRINCES OF THE ROYAL SECRET,

AT BERLIN, PARIS, AND BORDEAUX.

ARTICLE I.

No Lodge of Grand, Elect, Perfect and Sublime Masters can proceed to work, by electing officers or receiving candidates, unless warranted by a charter from the Sublime Princes of the Royal Secret, or from a Grand Inspector of the Order or his Deputy, duly signed and sealed, without which they are to be regarded as irregular, and their work declared null.

ARTICLE II.

No Lodge of Grand, Elect, Perfect and Sublime Masters can correspond with any other such Lodge, except such as are reported by the Secretary-General of the Grand Council to the Grand Inspector or his Deputy, and by him communicated.

ARTICLE III.

Whenever a Lodge of Perfection is made acquainted with the existence of another Lodge of Perfection, not included in the list furnished itself by the Grand Inspector or his Deputy, it should at once advise the Grand Inspector or his Deputy thereof, that it may be made known to the Grand Council.

ARTICLE IV.

If any brethren assemble irregularly, for the purpose of initiating persons into this degree, they should be reprimanded; and no Mason of a regular Lodge can recognize or visit them, on pain of such penalties as the laws of the Lodges of Perfection shall prescribe.

ARTICLE V.

Si une Loge Royale de Grand Élu Parfait et Sublime Maître, pour cause de mauvaise conduite excluoit un de ses membres, elle doit en donner immédiatement avis au Grand Inspecteur ou son Député pour qu'il le puisse transmettre aux Loges régulières ainsi qu'au Grand Conseil. Si une Loge régulière enfreignoit les loix, qui lui ont été imposées par l'engagement solemnel de nos Secrètes Constitutions, ou refusoit de se soumettre et de demander pardon de la manière la plus soumise par une pétition signée de tous ses membres, confessans leurs fautes, et en prouvant qu'ils ont cessés leurs travaux jusqu'à ce qu'il plût au Grand Conseil des Princes Sublimes de les rélever de leur interdiction, d'obtenir leur pardon, et de les faire rentrer en faveur.

ARTICLE VI.

Toutes les Loges régulières qui obtiendront de nouveaux Grades relatifs à l'ordre en général, doivent en donner avis immédiatement au Grand Inspecteur ou son Député.

ARTICLE VII.

Les présents Statuts et Règlemens doivent être lus à chaque frère, lorsqu'il reçoit le Grade de Royale Arche. Il promettra de les suivre exactement, et de reconnoître aussi en tous temps les Chevaliers d'Orient, Princes de Jérusalem, Chevaliers d'Orient et d'Occident, Chevaliers de l'Aigle Blanc, Chevalier de Rose Croix, Patriarche Noachite, Royale Hache, Grand Pontif, Chevaliers de l'Aigle Blanc et Noir et les Souverains Princes du Royal Secret, etc., ainsi que les Grands Inspecteurs et leurs Députés, pour leurs chefs, qu'ils promettent de respecter, et d'obéir à leurs conseils en ce qui leur sera prescrit. Ils doivent aussi promettre d'augmenter de zèle, ferveur et constance pour l'ordre, à fin de parvenir un jour au Grade de Grand Élu Parfait Maître Sublime, et enfin d'être soumis et obéissant aux Statuts et Règlemens présentement faits et à faire à l'avenir par les Princes Souverains, chefs de l'Ordre de la Maçonnerie, et leur rendront tous les honneurs qui leur sont prescrits ; et signeront une soumission en forme, pour donner plus de force à leur obligation.

ARTICLE V.

If a Royal Lodge of Grand, Elect, Perfect and Sublime Masters should expel one of its members for misconduct, information thereof must forthwith be given to the Grand Inspector or his Deputy, that he may be able to notify thereof the other regular Lodges and the Grand Council. If a regular Lodge should violate the laws imposed upon it by the solemn provisions of our Secret Constitutions, or should refuse to submit and to ask forgiveness in the most humble manner by a petition signed by all the members, confessing their fault, showing at the same time that they have ceased to work until such time as it shall please the Grand Council of the Sublime Princes to relieve them from interdict, to pardon them, and receive them again into favour.

ARTICLE VI.

Any new Lodge that may come into possession of new degrees, relating to the Order in general, should immediately make the same known to the Grand Inspector or his Deputy.

ARTICLE VII

The present Statutes and Regulations must be read to every Bro.·. when he takes the degree of Royal Arch. He must promise punctually to obey them, and at all times to recognize the Knights of the East, Princes of Jerusalem, Knights of the East and West, Knights of the White Eagle, Knights Rose Croix, Patriarchs Noachite, Knights of the Royal Axe, Grand Pontiffs, Knights Princes Adept, Knights of the White and Black Eagle, Sovereign Princes of the Royal Secret, and the Grand Inspectors and their Deputies, as his Chiefs, whom he must promise to respect, and their counsel to follow in whatever they direct. He must also promise to increase in zeal, fervour and constancy for the Order, to the end that he may one day attain to the degree of Grand, Elect, Perfect and Sublime Mason; and to be submissive and obedient to the Statutes and Regulations heretofore made, or that may hereafter be made by the Sovereign Princes, Chiefs of the Order of Masonry, and that he will pay them all the honours to which they are entitled: to add more force to such obligation, he must sign a submission in due form.

ARTICLE VIII.

Toutes les Loges de Grands Élus Parfaits Maîtres et Sublimes doivent être composées de neuf Officiers; le nombre général des fréres ne devant pas excéder celui de vingt-sept. Dans les neuf Officiers, le Trois-Fois-Parfait n'est pas compris. Il représente Salomon. Hiram, Roi de Tyr, est à sa droite, en l'absence du Grand Inspecteur ou son Député.

1o. A droite,* le Grand Garde des Sceaux, représentant Galaad, fils de Sophonia, chef des Lévites.

2o. Le Grand Trésorier, représentant Guibulum, confident de Salomon, devant la table des pains de proposition.

3o. Le Grand Orateur, représentant Abdamon, auprès de la table des parfums, au Nord, celui qui expliqua plusieurs énigmes à Salomon, et expliqua les caractères hiéroglyphes gravés sur des pièces de marbre trouvées dans les anciennes ruines d'Enoch, sur la montagne Acheldama.

4o. Le Grand Secrétaire, favori des deux Rois alliés, représentant Joabert, placé au Sud, vis à vis la table des parfums.

5o. A l'Occident, le premier Grand Surveillant Adonhiram, fils d'Abda, Prince Harodin du Liban, qui, après la mort d'H . . . . Ab. . . , eut l'inspection des travaux du Liban, et fut le premier des sept Maîtres Secrets.

6o. A l'Occident, à gauche du premier Grand Surveillant, le second Grand Surveillant, représentant Mahabon, le plus zélé Maître de son temps, grand ami d'H. . . Ab. . .

7o. Au Nord, le Grand Maître des Cérémonies, représentant Stolkin, un des trois qui découvrirent les neuf Arches et le Delta.

8o. Entre les deux Grands Surveillants, le Capitaine des Gardes, qui représente Bendia ou Zerbal, qui avait cet emploi quand les deux Rois firent alliance.

9o. Un Tuilleur, ou deux, pour que la Loge soit bien gardée.

ARTICLE IX.

On doit procéder une fois chaque année à l'élection du nouveau trois-fois-Puissant, et des nouveaux Officiers. Il n'y a qu'un Prince de Jérusalem qui puisse remplir la chaire. L'élection doit être faite

---

* ' A la gauche du trois fois Puissant;' Aveilhé's copy, which I follow in the translation, is evidently correct. The Order in which the Officers are named, is different in the two copies, and they vary in other respects. I have corrected the errors, as far as possible.

ARTICLE VIII.

Every Lodge of Grand, Elect, Perfect and Sublime Masons should have nine officers; including whom, the number of members should not exceed twenty-seven. The Th.·. Puissant is not counted among the nine officers. He represents Solomon. Hiram, King of Tyre, sits on his right, in the absence of the Grand Inspector or his Deputy.

1st. The Grand Keeper of the Seals, representing Galahad, son of Sophonia, Chief of the Levites, who sits on the left of the Th.·. Puissant.

2d. The Grand Treasurer, representing Guibulum, the confidant of Solomon, who sits in front of the table of shew-bread.

3d. The Grand Orator, representing Abdamon, who explained to Solomon many enigmas, and the hieroglyphics engraven on the pieces of marble found in the ancient ruins of Enoch on the mountain Aceldama; who sits near the Altar of Incense in the North.

4th. The Grand Secretary, representing Joabert, the favourite of the two allied Kings; who sits in the South; opposite the Altar of Incense.

5th. The Senior Grand Warden, representing Adonhiram, son of Abda, Prince Harodin of Libanus, who, after the death of H.... Ab...., was Inspector of the labourers on Mount Libanus, and the first of the Seven Secret Masters; who sits in the West.

6th. The Junior Grand Warden, representing Mahabon, the most zealous Master of his time, and a great friend of H.... Ab....; who sits in the West, on the left of the Senior Gr.·. Warden.

7th. The Grand Master of Ceremonies, representing Stolkin, one of the three who discovered the nine Arches and the Delta; who sits in the North.

8th. The Captain of the Guards, representing Bendia or Zerbal, who held that office during the alliance of the two kings, and who sits between the two Grand Wardens.

9th. One Tyler, or two, that the Lodge may be well guarded.

ARTICLE IX.

The Th.·. Puissant and other officers are to be elected every third year. No one but a Prince of Jerusalem can be elected to preside. The election is to be held on the 3d day of the 12th

le troisième du douzième mois, appellé Adar, qui répond au 21
Février, jour mémorable de l'année 2995, quand le précieux trésor
fut trouvé par trois zélés Maîtres Maçons, sous les ruines de notre
ancien Patriarche Enoch. La manière de choisir, soit les Officiers
ou le Candidat, dépend des loix particulières de la Loge, excepté
quand les Officiers sont choisis, ils doivent prêter leur obligation
au Grand Inspecteur ou son Député, de remplir leurs offices avec
zèle, constance, ferveur et affection envers leurs frères.

ARTICLE X.

Tout espèce de parti et de cabale est absolument défendu à l'é-
lection des officiers sous peine d'être exclus et d'avoir ses noms
rayés de l'Orient.

ARTICLE XI.

Tous les ff.˙. seront décorés en Loge de toutes leurs dignités.
Un frère qui entrera en Loge sans ses ornements ou l'enseigne
d'un degré supérieur, sera privé de sa voix pour cette fois, et paiera,
au trésor, l'amende que la Loge lui infligera.

ARTICLE XII.

Les Loges de Perfection doivent être tenues aux jours et heures
nommés, dont les frères composans la Loge auront régulièrement
avis par le Secrétaire, et d'avance, afin qu'en cas que quelques affaires de conséquence empêchassent quelques frères de s'y rendre,
ils puissent en donner avis le matin au Secrétaire par écrit, qui en
rendra compte à l'Assemblée du soir ; sous les peines que le trois-
fois-Puissant et la Loge prononcera.

ARTICLE XIII.

Toutes Loges de Grand Elu Parfait et Sublime Maçon doivent se
visiter par députation ou correspondance, le plus souvent possible,
et se procurer mutuellement toutes les lumières qu'elles acqué-
reront.

ARTICLE XIV.

Le Grand Secrétaire délivrera à chaque F.˙. en cas de voyage,
un certificat signé par le trois-fois-Puissant, les Surveillants et le

month, called Adar, which answers to the 21st of February, that
memorable day of the year 2995, when the precious treasure was
found by three zealous Master Masons under the ruins of our ancient
patriarch Enoch.   The mode of electing either of the officers or a
candidate depends on the particular Laws of the Lodge ; but when
the officers have been elected, they must take an obligation, to the
Grand Inspector or his Deputy, that they will perform the duties
of their office with zeal, constancy, fervour, and affection towards
their brethren.

ARTICLE X.

Every thing like party organization and cabal is absolutely pro-
hibited in connection with the election of officers, on pain of expul-
sion and erasure of membership.

ARTICLE XI.

All the Brethren must in open Lodge wear all their decorations.
A Bro∴ who enters a Lodge without his ornaments or the insignia
of some higher degree shall lose his right to vote at that meeting,
and pay into the Treasury such fine as the Lodge shall impose.

ARTICLE XII.

Lodges of Perfection are to be held on specified days and at fixed
hours, whereof the Brothers shall have due and regular notice from
the Secretary, in order that if business of importance prevents any
Bro∴ from attending, he may advise the Secretary thereof by letter on the morning of the day of meeting ; whereof the Secretary
shall inform the Lodge in the evening.   This the Brethren shall
not omit, under such penalties as the Th∴ Puissant and the Lodge
may determine.

ARTICLE XIII.

All Lodges of Grand, Elect, Perfect and Sublime Masons must
mutually visit each other, by deputations or correspondence, as frequently as possible, and communicate to each other whatever light
they may acquire.

·ARTICLE XIV.

The Grand Secretary shall issue to every Brother who is about
to travel, a certificate signed by the Th∴ Puissant, the Wardens,

Grand Garde des Sceaux, qui y fixera le sceau de la Loge, et contresigné du Grand Secrétaire. La signature du Fr∴ qui le reçoit sera apposée en marge.

ARTICLE XV.

Les Grands Élus Parfaits et Sublimes Maçons peuvent recevoir les ff∴ qui en sont dignes, et qui ont remplis des dignités dans les Loges Symboliques, dans tous les Grades qui précèdent la Perfection, tels que le Maître Secret, le Maître Parfait, le Secrétaire Intime, Prévôt et Juge, Intendant des Bâtiments, Élu des Neuf Élu des Quinze, Chevalier Illustre, Grand Maître Architecte, [et] Chevalier de Royale Arche. Le trois-fois-Puissant peut donner trois Grades en même temps à chaque frère, en récompense de son zèle ; et enfin le Grand Élu Parfait et Sublime Maçon, lorsque le temps sera accompli.

ARTICLE XVI.

Outre les Jours de fête du 24 Juin et 27 Décembre, le Grand Élu Parfait et Sublime Maçon célébrera chaque année la réédification du Premier Temple du Seigneur, le 5 octobre. Le plus ancien Prince et le plus haut en grade présidera, et les deux Surveillants-s'ils sont les moins anciens, seront remplacés par les plus anciens en grades, que le Président nommera ; ainsi dans le même ordre tous les autres Officiers.

ARTICLE XVII.

Toutes pétitions quelconques seront faites par un Grand Élu Parfait et Sublime Maçon, et alors les plus jeunes donneront leur avis ; et quand un candidat sera proposé en Loge, il faut qu'il soit reconnu avoir du respect et de l'attachement à sa religion, d'une vraie probité et discrétion, et qu'il ait donnés des preuves de son zèle, ferveur et constance pour l'Ordre et ses frères.

ARTICLE XVIII.

Lorsque les Surveillants sont avertis par le trois-fois-Puissant de son intention de tenir Loge, ils doivent l'assister, et contribuer de toute leur puissance au bonheur de la Loge ; et alors le Grand Maître des Cérémonies sera averti avant, pour préparer la Loge.

and the Grand Keeper of the Seals, who shall thereto affix the seal of the Lodge, and countersigned by the Grand Secretary. The signature of the brother to whom it is granted must appear in the margin.

ARTICLE XV.

The Grand, Elect, Perfect and Sublime Masons may admit to the degree of Perfection such brethren as are worthy thereof, and who have held office in Symbolic Lodges; and to all the degrees that precede those of Perfection, to wit, Secret Master, Perfect Master, Confidential Secretary, Provost and Judge, Intendant of the Buildings, Elect of the Nine, Elect of the Fifteen, Illustrious Knight, Grand Master Architect, and Knight of the Royal Arch. The Th.·. Puissant may confer three degrees at one and the same time on each Bro.·., by way of reward for zealous service; and may at last confer the degree of Grand, Elect, Perfect and Sublime Mason, when the proper time has elapsed.

ARTICLE XVI.

Besides the Feast-days of the 24th June and 27th December, the Grand, Elect, Perfect and Sublime Masons must every year, on the 5th of October, celebrate the rebuilding of the first Temple of the Lord. The Prince who is oldest and highest in degree will preside; and if the two Wardens be of inferior degree, their places will be filled by such brethren, higher in degree, as the President shall appoint : and so with all the other officers.

ARTICLE XVII.

All matters whatever must be proposed by a Grand, Elect, Perfect and Sublime Mason, and the members will vote in order, commencing with the youngest; and whenever a candidate is proposed to the Lodge, it must be shown that he respects and is attached to his religion, that he is a person of true probity and discretion, and that he has given proofs of his zeal, fervour and constancy for the Order and his brethren.

ARTICLE XVIII.

When the Wardens are notified by the Th.·. Puissant of his intention to hold a Lodge, they must attend, and with all their might advance the prosperity of the Lodge. The Master of Ceremonies must also be notified, in advance, that he may prepare the Hall.

5

ARTICLE X·X.

Le Grand Garde des Sceaux préparera les sceaux pour les réceptions, tiendra tout en ordre, et mettra les sceaux à tous les certificats ou autres pièces signés par les Officiers de la Loge.

ARTICLE XX.

Le Grand Orateur fera des discours à chaque réception et en même temps sur l'excellence de l'Ordre. Il instruira les nouveaux FF.·., leur expliquera les Mystères, les exhortera à continuer leur zèle, ferveur et constance, pour qu'ils puissent un jour arriver au grade de Grand, Élu, Parfait et Sublime Maçon. S'il a observé quelque indiscrétion dans les FF.·. ou quelques disputes entre eux, il en informera la Loge pour qu'on puisse travailler à leur réconciliation.

ARTICLE XXI.

Le Grand Trésorier gardera tous les fonds des charités ainsi que des réceptions, et il tiendra un livre de compte toujours prêt à être inspecté par la Loge ; et comme la charité est un devoir indispensable parmi les Maçons, les FF.·. doivent participer à ces fonds par des contributions volontaires selon leurs facultés.

ARTICLE XXII.

Le Grand Secrétaire tiendra un régistre de toutes les affaires, bien écrit, et toujours prêt à être inspecté par la Loge, le Grand Inspecteur ou son Député. Il enverra tous les ordres, donnés par le trois-fois-Puissant assez àtemps pour qu'ils puissent être remis avec certitude. Il doit préparer toutes les réquisitions à transmettre à la Loge, au Grand Conseil et au Grand Inspecteur ou son Député, ainsi que dans quelques parties étrangères, et il aura le plus grand soin de tenir les archives de son office dans le plus grand ordre.

ARTICLE XXIII.

Le Maître des Cérémonies doit être de bonne heure au Temple pour tout préparer, afin que les travaux ne soient pas retardés. Il est toujours un des examinateurs et introducteur de tous les visiteurs selon leurs grades. En conséquence, il doit être très instruit des dignités et avoir la confiance de la Loge.

ARTICLE XIX.

The Grand Keeper of the Seals will have the seals ready for receptions, set every thing in order, and affix the seals to all certificates or other documents signed by the Officers of the Lodge.

ARTICLE XX.

The Grand Orator will deliver a discourse at each reception, enlarging therein upon the excellence of the Order. He will instruct the new brethren, explain to them the Mysteries, and exhort them not to slacken in their zeal, fervour, and constancy, that they may attain to the degree of Grand, Elect, Perfect, and Sublime Mason. If he has noticed any indiscretions on the part of any brethren, or any disputes among them, he will advise the Lodge thereof, that it may endeavor to bring about a reconciliation.

ARTICLE XXI.

The Grand Treasurer will safely keep all funds devoted to charitable purposes, as well as moneys received for receptions. He will keep a regular book of accounts, at all times ready to be examined by the Lodge; and as Charity is an indispensable duty among Masons, the brethren should voluntarily contribute to the fund for that purpose, each according to his means.

ARTICLE XXII.

The Grand Secretary will keep a record of all the transactions of the Lodge, plainly written, and always ready to be inspected by the Lodge, the Grand Inspector or his Deputy. He will dispatch all orders issued by the Th∴ Puissant, within such time that they may reach their destination in due season. He must prepare all requisitions that are to be transmitted to the Lodge, to the Grand Council, the Grand Inspector, his Deputy, or into foreign countries; and he will take the greatest possible care to keep the business of his office in perfect order.

ARTICLE XXIII.

The Master of Ceremonies must repair to the Temple in due season, so as to have every thing ready, that the work may not be delayed. He is always one of the examiners of visiting brethren, and introduces them according to their degrees. Consequently he ought to be at all points instructed in the several degrees, and possess the confidence of the Lodge.

ARTICLE XXIV.

Le Capitaine des Gardes a l'inspection sur le Tuilleur. Il doit s'assurer si la Loge est bien couverte : il prend tous les visiteurs, avec son chapeau sur la tête et l'épée à la main, excepté pour les Princes Maçons, devant lesquels il doit avoir la tête découverte. Il avertira le trois-fois-Puissant lorsqu'un visiteur demandera à être admis, et assistera à son examen ; il précèdera toujours les FF.·. dans les cérémonies d'instruction ; et si le Capitaine des Gardes rapporte qu'un visiteur est Prince Maçon, il doit le recevoir avec tous les honnneurs, à l'effet de quoi, tous les FF.·. formeront une voûte avec leurs épées, et le Grand Maître des Cérémonies doit conduire le visiteur jusqu'au pied du trône, après quoi, il le conduit à un siége élevé près du trois-fois-Puissant.

ARTICLE XXV.

Si une Loge a méritée d'être dissoute ou interdite pendant un certain temps, les Officiers sont alors obligés de déposer leurs Constitutions, Règlemens, Statuts, ainsi que tous leurs papiers, au Grand Conseil, s'il y en a, et à ce défaut, entre les mains du Grand Inspecteur ou son Député, où ils resteront jusqu'à ce que la Loge ait obtenu grâce ; ou si les membres d'une telle Loge ne se soumettoient pas au décret du Grand Conseil, leur désobéissance, noms, degrés et qualités civiles seront transmis par écrit dans toutes les Loges connues sur les deux Hémisphères, pour encourir le mépris de tous les Maçons. Nous prions le Grand Architecte de l'Univers de prévenir de tels malheurs, et de nous inspirer dans le choix de bons frères pour la perfection de l'Ordre.

ARTICLE XXVI.

Si un membre d'une Loge, qui a été dissoute par le Grand Conseil, prouvoit, dans une pétition au Grand Conseil, qu'il est innocent, il aura grâce, et se joindra à une autre Loge constituée.

ARTICLE XXVII.

Rien de ce qui se fait en Loge ne doit être révélé hors de la Loge, qu'à aucun autre membre de la même Loge, sous les peines que la Loge infligera.

ARTICLE XXVIII.

Nul visiteur ne sera admis avant que la Loge soit ouverte, et qu'après avoir été scrupuleusement examiné par deux FF.·. ins-

ARTICLE XXIV.

The Captain of the Guards sees that the Tyler does his duty; and it is his business to see the Lodge well tyled. He receives all visitors, wearing his hat, and sword in hand, unless they are Princes Masons, in whose presence he is uncovered. He will advise the Th∴ Puissant whenever a visitor desires to be admitted, will assist in examining him, and will in all cases precede the brethren in the ceremonies of instruction. When he reports that the visitor is a Prince Mason, such visitor will be received with all the honours, the brethren forming the vault of steel with their swords, and the Grand Master of Ceremonies conducting him to the foot of the throne, and afterwards to an elevated seat near the Th∴ Puissant.

ARTICLE XXV.

If any Lodge is for good cause dissolved or temporarily interdicted, the Officers thereof must deposit the Charter, Regulations and Statutes, and all the papers of the Lodge, with the Grand Council, if there be one, and if not, with the Gr∴ Inspector or his Deputy; where they will remain until the Lodge is allowed to resume labour. And if the members of such Lodge should not submit to the decision of the Grand Council, their disobedience, with their names, degrees and civil characters, are to be notified in writing to all the recognized Lodges in the two Hemispheres, that they may incur the contempt of all Masons. May the Grand Architect of the Universe avert so great a misfortune, and inspire us to select good men for our brethren, that thereby the Order may attain perfection.

ARTICLE XXVI.

If a member of a Lodge that has been dissolved by the Grand Council, shows that body by petition that he is innocent, he shall be restored to favour, and affiliated with another Lodge.

ARTICLE XXVII.

Nothing that is done in a Lodge should be made known out of the Lodge, except to a member of the same, under such penalty as the Lodge shall inflict.

ARTICLE XXVIII.

No visitor can be admitted until the Lodge is opened, nor until he has been scrupulously examined by two well-informed brethren;

truits ; et il prêtera son obligation, à moins que quelques membres de la Loge n'affirment avoir vu le frère visiteur dans une Loge régulièrement constituée, et de ce grade au moins.

ARTICLE XXIX.

Chaque Loge peut avoir deux FF∴ Tuilleurs. Leurs mœurs doivent être connues. Ils seront décorés aux dépens de la Loge, et porteront leurs attributs seulement à la boutonnière de leur habit.

ARTICLE XXX.

Les Chevaliers et Princes Maçons étant les grands lumières de la Loge, si aucunes plaintes étoient faites contre l'un d'eux, elles seront faites par écrit, et présentées dans la Loge prochaine, qui les écoutera et en décidera ; et si une des parties se croyait lézée, elle aura la liberté d'en appeler au Grand Conseil, dont la détermination sera finale et décisive.

ARTICLE XXXI.

Le secret dans nos Mystères étant d'obligation indispensable, le trois-fois-Puissant Grand Maître, avant de fermer chaque Loge, recommandera ce devoir aux FF∴ dans la manière et forme d'usage.

ARTICLE XXXII.

Si un frère étoit malade et qu'un membre le scut, il en donnera au plustôt avis au trois-fois-Puissant pour qu'il puisse recevoir les secours dont il aurait besoin ; et le G∴ Hospitalier aura soin de le voir pour s'assurer s'il est bien soigné.

ARTICLE XXXIII.

Si un F∴ mouroit, tous les FF∴ seront obligés d'assister à ses funérailles de la manière accoutumée.

ARTICLE XXXIV.

Si un F∴ est dans l'infortune, il est du devoir de chaque frère de l'assister.

ARTICLE XXXV.

Si le trois-fois-Puissant n'étoit pas présent en Loge, une heure après celle fixée pour l'assemblée, et qu'il y eût cinq frères présens,

and he shall take his obligation also, unless more than one member of the Lodge shall state that they have seen him sit in a regularly constituted Lodge of at least the degree of that which he seeks to visit.

ARTICLE XXIX.

Every Lodge may have two Tylers ; whose good character should be known. They will be clothed at the expense of the Lodge, and wear the proper jewel at the button-hole of their coat.

ARTICLE XXX.

The Knights and Princes Masons being the great lights of the Lodge, all complaints against them shall be made in writing and presented at the next Lodge-meeting. The Lodge shall hear and decide ; and if a party thinks himself aggrieved, he may appeal to the Grand Council, which shall determine in the last resort.

ARTICLE XXXI.

Secrecy as to the Mysteries being of indispensable obligation, the Th∴ P∴ Grand Master shall, before closing any Lodge, inculcate that duty on the Brethren in the usual manner and form.

ARTICLE XXXII.

If a brother be sick, any member knowing thereof must forthwith inform the Th∴ Puissant, in order that he may receive the necessary attention ; and the Bro∴ Hospitaller must visit him, to see that he is properly cared for.

ARTICLE XXXIII.

When a brother dies, all the brethren are obliged to attend his funeral in the usual manner.

ARTICLE XXXIV.

If a brother meet with misfortunes, it is the duty of every brother to visit him.

ARTICLE XXXV.

If the Th∴ Puissant be not present at a Lodge meeting, for one hour after the time fixed for opening, and there be five brethren

le plus ancien Officier remplira immédiatement le trône, et procé-
dera régulièrement aux travaux, pourvu que le Grand Inspecteur
ou son Député soient absens ; mais s'il est présent, il sera invité à
remplir le trône avec tous les honneurs, et en son absence, les
mêmes honneurs seront rendus à son Député.

ARTICLE XXXVI.

Pour établir la régularité dans la Loge, le trois-fois-Puissant
Maître et le Grand Inspecteur ou son Député doivent avoir un
tableau de tous les membres de la Loge, des grades et des qualités
civiles, pour les présenter devant le Grand Conseil, et les transmettre à toutes les Loges régulières. Ils informeront aussi le Grand
Inspecteur ou son Député de toutes les nouvelles matières qui seront communiquées à la Loge.

ARTICLE XXXVII.

Si les membres de la Loge pensent nécessaire de faire quelques
altérations aux présentes Constitutions et Règlemens, cela ne pourra
être que par pétition par écrit, présentée avant à la Loge, avant la
fête annuelle ; et si les membres, après avoir mûrement considérés
l'objet mis en question comme n'étant pas contraire auxdits Statuts
et Règlemens, l'écrit sera communiqué au Grand Conseil des Princes, et s'ils l'approuvent, il sera envoyé au Grand Inspecteur ou son
Député du District, qui décidera l'objet proposé, sans altérer aucunes de nos anciennes coutumes, obligations ou cérémonies, ou di-
minuer la force de notre présente Constitution ou Règlement, sous
peines d'interdiction. Aussi toutes les Loges de Grand, Elu, Parfait
et Sublime Maçon et Anciens Maçons, régulièrement établies sous
notre protection, se gouverneront et se dirigeront elles-mêmes à
l'avenir, dans tous les lieux de la terre où notre Ordre sera établi
de cette manière, et seront dirigées par l'Inspecteur, son Député ou
Prince Maçon soit en particulier ou dans le Grand Conseil, s'il y
en a un ; et pour y donner la première force et existence, nous
avons résolus de créer des Inspecteurs et Députés Inspecteurs,
qui voyageront par mer et par terre, pour notifier et observer, dans
toutes les Loges régulièrement constituées : copie desquelles loix
et règlemens seront délivrées par [à] nos dits Commissaires, Députés Inspecteurs, avec des titres authentiques et pouvoirs en
forme, pour être connus et autorisés dans leurs fonctions.

present, the oldest Officer will for the time take the throne, and proceed regularly with the work, provided that the Grand Inspector and his Deputy are absent; but if either of them be present, he shall be invited to take the throne, with all the honours; the same honours being paid the Deputy as to the Inspector, in the absence of the latter.

ARTICLE XXXVI.

To secure regularity in the Lodge, the Th.·. P.·. Master and the Gr.·. Inspector or his Deputy must keep a list of all the members of the Lodge, showing the degree and civil character of each, to be laid before the Gr.·. Council and transmitted to all the regular Lodges. They will also advise the Grand Inspector or his Deputy of every matter of interest communicated to the Lodge.

ARTICLE XXXVII.

If the members of any Lodge deem it necessary to make any alterations in the present Constitutions and Regulations, that can only be done by petition in writing, presented to the Lodge prior to the annual Feast. If the members, upon mature consideration of the matter proposed, find nothing therein contrary to said Statutes and Regulations, the proposition in writing shall be transmitted to the Grand Council of the Princes, and if they approve it, it shall be sent to the Gr.·. Inspector or his Deputy for the District, who shall decide thereon; none of our ancient customs, obligations or ceremonies being changed, nor the force of our present Constitutions and Regulations diminished, on pain of interdiction. Wherefore all Lodges of Grand, Elect, Perfect and Sublime Masons and of Ancient Masons, regularly established under our protection shall so govern and direct themselves for the future, in every place in the world where our Order is established, being under the direction of the Inspector, his Deputy or the Princes Masons, individually or in Grand Council, if there be one: Whereto to give force and actuality, we have resolved to create Inspectors and Deputy Inspectors, who shall travel by land and sea, to take note and observe in all Lodges regularly constituted. A copy of which Laws and Regulations shall be delivered to our aforesaid Delegates, Deputy Inspectors, with authentic patents and powers in due form, that they may be recognized and duly empowered in the exercise of their functions.

AINSI DÉCRÉTÉ par nos Chefs et Dignes Protecteurs dans leurs légitimes Assemblées, vraie Science et pleine Puissance, comme représentant du Souverain des Souverains.

FAIT au Grand O.˙. de Paris, Berlin et Bordeaux dans un lieu Saint, sous la Voûte Céleste, près du B.˙. A.˙., le 25 Juin, du 7me mois, de l'an 1762, et transmis au T.˙. Ill.˙. et T.˙. Puissant Prince Etienne Morin, Grand Inspecteur de toutes les Loges régulières dans le nouveau monde.

AU Grand O.˙. de Berlin, sous la Voute Céleste, le jour et an susdits, et certifié par nous, Grand Inspecteurs Généraux et Députés, le 22 Décembre 1768. *Signé :* ETIENNE MORIN, MOSES COHEN, et SPITZER et HYMAN ISAAC LONG, qui l'a déposé; et certifié conforme aux Archives du Grand Conseil Sublime à l'Orient de Charleston, Caroline du Sud. Pour copie sincère et véritable.

J'N B'TE M'IE DELAHOGUE,

Député Gd. Insp. G'l P'ce M'on,

Souv. Gd. Commandeur du Gd. Conseil

Sublime, Orient de Charleston, C'ne du Sud.

A'DRE F. AUGUSTE DE GRASSE,

Grand Garde des Sceaux et Archives.

Le certificat dans le livre d'*Aveilhé* est comme suit :

"FAIT au Grand Orient de Bordeaux et Paris, dans un lieu Saint et Secret, sous la voûte Céleste, près le B.˙. A.˙., le 25 du septième mois de l'année 1762, et transmis au très respectable et très excellent ETIENNE MORIN, Grand Inspecteur de toutes les Loges régulièrement constituées dans le nouveau monde.

AU Grand Orient de Bordeaux, sous la Voûte Céleste, les jour et an susdits, et certifié par nous, Grand Inspecteur et Député, le 22 Décembre 1762.

NOUS, Soussignés Députés Inspecteurs Généraux et Princes Maçons, etc., etc., etc. certifions que les Statuts et Règlemens transcrits ci-dessus et des autres parts, et donnés par LA GRANDE LOGE ET SOUVERAIN GRAND CONSEIL des Sublimes Princes de la Maçonnerie, au Grand Orient de France, au très puissant et respectable frère ETIENNE MORIN, sont conformes à l'original, dont il a transmis copie au très respectable frère FRANKIN, Député Grand Inspecteur en l'isle de la Jamaïque, et encore conformes à la copie duement en forme qu'on a remis dans les Archives de la Loge Sublime à l'Orient de Charleston, le très respectable frère HYMAN

So DECREED by our Chiefs and Worthy Protectors in lawful assembly of true science and ample power as Representatives of the Sovereign of the Sovereigns.

DONE, at the Grand Orient of Paris, Berlin and Bordeaux, in a Holy place, under the Celestial Vault, near the B.·. B.·., the 25th day of the 7th month of the year 1762; and transmitted to the Very Ill.·. and Very Puissant Prince Stephen Morin, Grand Inspector of all the regular Lodges in the new world.

AT the Grand Orient of Berlin, under the Celestial Vault, the day and year above mentioned, and certified by us, Grand Inspectors General and Deputies, the 22d December, 1768. *Signed:* ETIENNE MORIN, MOSES COHEN, SPITZER and HYMAN ISAAC LONG; by the last of whom it is deposited: and certified to agree with the archives of the Grand Sublime Council at the Orient of Charleston, South Carolina. A true and correct copy.

J'N B'TE M'IE DELAHOGUE,
Dep.·. Gr.·. Insp.·. Gen.·. P'ce Mason.
Sov.·. Gr.·. Com.·. of the Gr.·. and Sub.·.
Council, at the O.·. in Charleston, So,·. Car.·.

A'DRE F. AUGUSTE DE GRASSE,
Grand Keeper of the Seals and Archives.

The certificate in AVEILHE's copy is as follows:

" DONE at the Grand Orient of Bordeaux and Paris, in a holy and secret place, under the Celestial Vault, near the B.·. B.·., the 25th of the 7th month of the year 1762, and transmitted to the Very Resp.·. and Very Exc.·. STEPHEN MORIN, Grand Inspector of all Lodges in the new world.

AT the Gr. O.·. of Bordeaux, under the Celestial Vault, the day and year aforesaid, and certified by us, Grand Inspector and Deputy, the 22d December, 1762.

WE, the undersigned, Deputies Inspectors Generals and Princes Masons, etc., etc., etc., do certify that the Statutes and Regulations above and herein before transcribed, and given by THE GRAND LODGE AND SOVEREIGN GRAND COUNCIL of the Sublime Princes of Masonry, at the Grand Orient of Paris to the Very Puissant and Very Respectable Brother, STEPHEN MORIN, conform to the original, whereof he transmitted a copy to the Very Resp.·. Bro.·. FRANKIN, Deputy Grand Inspector for the Island of Jamaica; and that they also conform to the copy in due form, deposited in the archives of the Sublime Lodge at the O.·. of Charleston, by the

Isaac Long, lorsqu'il l'a constituée ; en foi de quoi nous avons signé, et pour plus grande authenticité avons apposé au bas du présent le sceau de nos armes, et le grand sceau des Princes Maçons.

A l'Orient de Charleston, Caroline du Sud, le 9eme jour du 4me mois appellé Tammuz, de l'année 5557, de la Restauration, et de l'ère Vulgaire, le 9 Juin 1797.

[*Signés :* Delahogue, Souverain, etc., H. I. Long, Robin, de Grasse, Saint Paul et Petit, tous *comme* Députés Inspecteurs Généraux et Princes Maçons ; avec certificat du frère Aveilhé, du 10 Décembre 1797, et de Delahogue, avec deux sceaux, l'un d'eux du Sublime Grand Conseil, et l'autre je ne connois pas. *Vu* par Auguste de Grasse, K. H. P. R. S. Souv∴ Gr∴ Insp. Gen. du 33e degré, etc., à Charleston, le 12 Mars 5802.]

DEVOIRS ET PRIVILÉGES

DES

Princes de Rose Croix ou Chevaliers de l'Aigle ou du Pelican.

Les Princes de Rose Croix ont droit de tenir le maillet dans toutes les Loges Symboliques où ils se présentent. Ils prennent place à côté du Vénérable, et si cet honneur ne leur étoit pas offert, ils se placeroient après le dernier apprentif, en signe d'humilité.

Ils ne doivent signer aucunes pièces maçonniques, sans les caractères qui désignent leur grade. Lorsqu'il y a un Chapitre réglé dans un endroit, il doit s'assembler d'obligation six fois par an.

Le Jeudi Saint,

Le Jour de Pâques,

Le Jeudi d'après Pâques,

Le Jour de l'Ascension,

Le Jour de la Pentecôte,

Et le jour de la Toussaint, indépendamment des deux fêtes de la Saint Jean.

Very Resp.·. Bro.·. HYMAN ISAAC LONG, when he established that body. In faith whereof we have signed these presents, and for greater authenticity do affix below the Seal of our arms and the Great Seal of the Princes Masons.

AT the Orient of Charleston, South Carolina, the 9th day of the 4th Month, called Tammuz, of the year of the Restoration, 5557, and of the Vulgar Era, the 9th of June, 1797.

[Signed by DELAHOGUE, Sovereign, LONG, ROBIN, DE GRASSE, ST. PAUL and PETIT, as Deputy Inspectors General and Princes Masons; with certificate of Bro.·. AVEILHE, dated 10th December, 1797, and of DELAHOGUE, with two seals, one that of the Sub.·. Gr.· Council, and the other not known to me. *Visé* by AUGUSTE DE GRASSE, K. H. P. R. S., Sov. Gr.·. Insp.·. Gen.·. of the 33d degree, &c., Charleston, 12th March, 5802].

DUTIES AND PRIVILEGES

OF THE

Princes Rose Croix, or Knights of the Eagle or the Pelican.

The Princes of Rose Croix are entitled to take the mallet in any Symbolic Lodges at which they are present. They sit by the side of the Ven.·., and if that honour is not offered them, they take their place behind the youngest apprentice, in token of their humility.

They must sign no Masonic document, without adding the characters that indicate their degree. When a Chapter is regularly established any where, it must of necessity meet six times a year, to wit:

On Holy [or Maundy] Thursday,
On Easter day,
On the Thursday after Easter,
On Ascension day,
On the day of Pentecost,
And on All-Saints' Day; besides meeting on the two feast-days of the Saint John.

Un Chapitre ne peut être constitué à moins de trois. Lorsqu'il est plus nombreux, il a les mêmes Officiers qu'une Loge ordinaire, et les élections s'y font le Jeudi d'après Pâques.

Les Chevaliers de Rose Croix sont obligés à la charité envers les pauvres, visiter les prisoniers, les malades, les secourir dans leurs besoins, selon ses facultés.

Lorsqu'un Rose Croix meurt, on doit l'enterrer avec son cordon : les Chevaliers présents doivent assister à son convoi, avec leurs décorations sous l'habit, si elles ne peuvent être portées sans scandale. On doit faire un service au défunt dans le Chapitre, où l'on doit prononcer son oraison funèbre.

Les Chevaliers ne peuvent se battre les uns contre les autres.

Ils ne peuvent se dispenser de se rendre aux invitations du Chapitre, que pour cause de maladie.

Le Chapitre doit être éclairé avec des bougies jaunes ou de l'huile d'olive. Un Chevalier de Rose Croix ne peut être tuilé lorsqu'il se présente en Loge ; aussi doit-il être pour cela muni d'un brévet particulier qui déclare son grade. Il doit en porter le bijou dans toutes les Loges.

CERTIFIÉ conforme à l'original, déposé aux Archives du Grand Conseil des Princes du Royal Secret, à l'Orient de Charleston, Caroline du Sud.

J'N B'TE M'IE DELAHOGUE,
Député Gd. Insp. G'l et P'ce M'on,
Souverain Gd. Command. du Conseil Sublime.

A'DRE F. AUGUSTE DE GRASSE,
Grand Garde des Sceaux et Archives.
[Avec les deux sceaux.]

La copie d'*Aveilhé* est certifié par DELAHOGUE, LONG, ROBIN, DE GRASSE, SAINT PAUL et PETIT, le 9 Juin 1797 ; et par AVEILHÉ, le 10 Décembre 1797, et *vu* par DE GRASSE, à Charleston, le 12 Mars 1802.

A Chapter cannot consist of less than three members. When there are more, it has the same Officers as an ordinary Lodge; and the elections are held on the Thursday after Easter.

The Knights Rose Croix are bound to give charity to the poor, to visit those in prison and the sick, and to give them aid in their necessities, each according to his means.

When a Knight Rose Croix dies, he is to be buried with his collar. All Knights in the place must attend the burial, wearing their insignia under their coats, if they cannot openly display them without scandal. A Funeral Service must be performed in the Chapter, at which an oration in memory of the deceased will be delivered.

The Knights cannot engage in mortal combat one with the other.

They cannot be excused for non-attendance at meetings of the Chapter, when notified, except in case of sickness.

The Chapter must be lighted with candles of yellow wax, or lamps fed with olive oil.

A Knight Rose Croix is not to be tyled, when he presents himself for admission into a Lodge as a visitor. He should therefore have a special brief, evidencing his rank. He must wear his jewel in all Lodges.

CERTIFIED to conform to the original in the archives of the Grand Council of the Princes of the Royal Secret, at the Orient of Charleston, South Carolina.

J'N B'TE M'IE DELAHOGUE,

Dep∴ Gr∴ Insp∴ Gen∴ and P'ce Mason,

Sov∴ Gr∴ Commander of the Sub∴ Council.

A'DRE AUGUSTE DE GRASSE,

Grand Keeper of the Seals and Archives.

[With two Seals.]

The copy of AVEILHE is certified by DELAHOGUE, LONG, ROBIN, DE GRASSE, SAINT PAUL and PETIT, the 9th June, 1797; and by AVEILHE, the 10th December, 1797; and *viséd* by DE GRASSE, at Charleston, the 12th March, 1802.

STATUTS, RÈGLEMENS, DEVOIRS ET PRIVILÉGES

Princes de Jerusalem.

ARTICLE I.

Les Princes de Jérusalem sont les Chefs de la Maçonnerie. Ils ont le droit de visiter et d'inspecter les Loges, jusqu'au Conseil des Chevaliers d'Orient. Ils peuvent casser et révoquer les travaux, s'ils sont contraires aux Loix Maçonniques.

ARTICLE II.

Quand un Prince de Jérusalem visite une Loge ou un Conseil, il doit être décoré du bijou et des ornemens de son ordre, et s'annoncer comme Prince de Jérusalem.

ARTICLE III.

Le Vénérable doit députer un F∴ de ce grade, s'il y en a, pour aller l'examiner. Quand il l'a fait, il retourne pour en rendre compte à la Loge, et l'annoncer en sa qualité. Si c'est un Conseil, le Souverain ordonne que les deux battans de la porte soient ouverts pour former la voûte d'acier, et faire placer le visiteur à sa droite.

Si c'est dans une Loge Symbolique, le Vénérable députe quatre frères pour aller le recevoir, en observant que ce ne doit jamais être les Officiers dignitaires, qui ne doivent jamais quitter leurs places. Ces députés vont chercher le visiteur, le conduisent à la porte, dont on ouvre les deux battans, on forme la voûte d'acier, et il est conduit à la place la plus éminente, et si le Vénérable n'est pas Prince de Jérusalem, il lui offre son maillet et sa place, qu'il est libre d'accepter ou de refuser. Les mêmes cérémonies ont lieu lorsqu'il sort du Temple.

STATUTES, REGULATIONS, DUTIES AND PRIVILEGES

OF THE

Princes of Jerusalem.

ARTICLE I.

The Princes of Jerusalem are the Chiefs of Masonry. They have the right to visit and inspect Lodges, up to the degree of Knights of the East: and may quash and recall their work, if it be contrary to the laws of Masonry.

ARTICLE II.

When a Prince of Jerusalem visits a Lodge or Council, he should wear the jewel and ornaments of his degree, and announce himself as a Prince of Jerusalem.

ARTICLE III.

The Ven∴ will deputize a Bro∴ of that degree, if there be one, to go out and examine him. When he has so done, he returns, reports to the Lodge, and announces the Visitor by his rank.

If this is in a Council, the Sovereign orders the folding-doors to be thrown open, that the Vault of Steel may be formed, and the Visitor seated on his right. If in a symbolic Lodge, the Ven∴ delegates four brethren to go and receive him, never selecting the officers, dignitaries, who must not leave their stations. The Delegates go to the Visitor and conduct him to the entrance. The folding-doors are thrown open, the Vault of Steel is formed, and he is conducted to the most honourable seat; and the Venerable, if he be not himself a Prince of Jerusalem, offers him his mallet and his seat, which he may accept or refuse as he pleases. The same ceremonies are to be observed when he retires from the Temple.

6

Si un Prince de Jérusalem se présente à une Loge où il n'y a aucun frère de ce grade, et sans certificat, on députe le frère le plus expert, et le Vénérable même, s'il est jugé nécessaire, pour aller l'examiner et s'assurer de ses connoissances. Après cet examen, il doit donner sa parole d'honneur qu'il est Prince de Jérusalem, ainsi qu'il est porté par l'article 2.

ARTICLE IV.

Le Conseil des Princes de Jérusalem, se nomme Conseil des Très Vaillans et Très Illustres Princes. Toutes les Loges inférieures sont obligées de leur rendre compte de leur travaux ; et ils ont le droit d'examiner leurs Constitutions, sans que personne puisse s'en formaliser. Les Princes de Jérusalem, au nombre de cinq, sont Juges en dernier ressort des délibérations des Loges ; et quand ils ont prononcé leur sentence, il n'y a point d'appel. Ils tiennent ce pouvoir de leurs prédécesseurs, auxquels le peuple de Jérusalem le conféra. Ils ont la tête couverte en Loge, et parlent au Vénérable sans lui demander la parole.

ARTICLE V.

Les droits des Princes de Jérusalem leur ayant été accordés comme récompense des services qu'ils ont rendus au peuple de Jérusalem, leurs profondes connaissances, et les obligations que leur a la Maçonnerie, leur a mérité d'être les égaux du Grand Prince Zorobabel de la race de David.

ARTICLE VI.

Les Princes de Jérusalem doivent être honnêtes, justes, polis et strictes observateurs des loix, en faisant rendre la justice, et en faisant observer le bon ordre dans les Loges.

ARTICLE VII.

Si les Princes de Jérusalem ne mènent pas une vie irréprochable, ou qu'ils manquent à la probité, ils seront punis par les Princes de Jérusalem, et à la majorité.

ARTICLE VIII.

Si un Prince de Jérusalem en tourne un autre en ridicule, ou se moque de lui, il sera privé d'assister à trois Conseils consécutifs.

If a Prince of Jerusalem applies to visit a Lodge in which there is no brother of that degree, and without his certificate, the most expert Bro.·. is delegated, and the Ven.·. himself, if need be, to go out and examine him, and satisfy themselves of his proficiency. After this examination, he must give his word of honour that he is a Prince of Jerusalem, as is provided by Art. 2.

ARTICLE IV.

A Council of Princes of Jerusalem is styled ' Council of the Very Valiant and Very Illustrious Princes.' All inferior Lodges must report to them their work; and they have the right to examine their charters, without any one taking offence thereat. The Princes of Jerusalem, to the number of five, are the judges in the last resort of the decisions of the Lodges, there being no appeal from their judgments. They derive this power from their predecessors, on whom the people of Jerusalem conferred it. They sit covered in Lodges, and address the Ven.·. without asking permission.

ARTICLE V.

The rights of the Princes of Jerusalem having been granted them as a reward for the services rendered by them to the people of Jerusalem, for their profound knowledge and the obligations under which they laid Masonry, they are deservedly the equals of the great Prince Zerubbabel, of the race of David.

ARTICLE VI.

Princes of Jerusalem should be honourable and just men, courteous, and strict observers of the laws, seeing justice done, and enforcing good order in the Lodges.

ARTICLE VII.

If any Prince of Jerusalem does not lead an irreproachable life, or acts dishonestly, he is to be punished by the other Princes by majority of votes.

ARTICLE VIII.

If a Prince of Jerusalem ridicules another, or derides him, he shall be forbidden to sit at three successive Councils.

ARTICLE IX.

Si un Prince de Jérusalem en appelle un autre en duel, il sera exclu du Conseil, son nom biffé, et avis en sera donné au Grand Conseil, à tous les Conseils de la correspondance, et à toutes les Loges Symboliques.

ARTICLE X.

Si, à une élection d'Officiers, un Prince de Jérusalem sollicite des voix en sa faveur ou pour quelqu'autre, il sera exclus pour jamais.

ARTICLE XI.

La Grande Fête des Princes de Jérusalem est le 23me jour du 12me mois, en mémoire des actions de grâces qui furent rendues ce jour à Dieu, pour la reconstruction du Temple. C'est ce jour que se font les élections des Officiers de tous les Conseils de Princes de Jérusalem.

Le 20me jour du 10me mois, doit aussi se célébrer la fête de l'Ordre en commémoration de l'entrée triomphante des Ambassadeurs à Jérusalem, à leur retour de Babylone.

ARTICLE XII.

Un Conseil de Prince de Jérusalem, doit être composé au moins de cinq. Le Souverain représente Zorobabel.

Les deux Surveillants sont nommés Très Eclairés. Les Officiers sont comme dans les autres Loges, et tous se nomment Illustres.

CERTIFIÉ conforme à l'original, déposé aux Archives du Grand Conseil, à l'Orient Sublime de Charleston, Caroline du Sud.

[*Signé* par DELAHOGUE et DE GRASSE, comme les Statuts, et avec les deux Sceaux.]

La copie d'*Aveilhé* est certifiée par DELAHOGUE, LONG, ROBIN, DE GRASSE, SAINT PAUL et PETIT, le 9 Juin 1797, et par AVEILHÉ, le 10 Décembre 1797, et *vu* par DE GRASSE, à Charleston, le 12 Mars, 5802.

ARTICLE IX.

If a Prince of Jerusalem challenges another to fight a duel, he is to be expelled from his Council, his name erased, and notice thereof given to the Grand Council, to all corresponding Councils, and to all the Symbolic Lodges.

ARTICLE X.

If at any election of officers, a Prince of Jerusalem solicits votes for himself or any other person, he shall be forever expelled.

ARTICLE XI.

The Grand Feast of the Princes of Jerusalem is the 23d day of the 12th month, in memory of the thank-offerings that day rendered to God, for the rebuilding of the Temple. On that day the elections of Officers of all Councils of Princes of Jerusalem are to be held.

On the 20th day of the 10th month, also, a Feast of the Order is to be celebrated in commemoration of the triumphal entry into Jerusalem of the Ambassadors on their return from Babylon.

ARTICLE XII.

A Council of Princes of Jerusalem must be composed of at least five. The Sovereign represents Zerubbabel. The two Wardens are styled 'Very Enlightened.' The Officers are as in other Lodges, and are all styled 'Illustrious.'

CERTIFIED to conform to the original deposited in the Archives of the Grand Council, at the Sub∴ O∴ of Charleston, South Carolina.

[*Signed* by DELAHOGUE and DE GRASSE, like the Statutes; and with two Seals.]

The Copy of *Aveilhé* is certified by DELAHOGUE, LONG, ROBIN, DE GRASSE, SAINT-PAUL, and PETIT, the 9th June, 1797; and by AVEILHÉ, the 10th of December, 1797; and *visé* by DE GRASSE, at Charleston, 12th March, 1802.

STATUTS ET RÈGLEMENS GÉNÉRAUX

DES

Chevaliers D'Orient.

ARTICLE I.

Le Conseil des Chevaliers d'Orient sera composé du Souverain, du Garde des Sceaux, du Général, du Grand Trésorier du Ministre d'Etat, et de tous les FF∴ Chevaliers reçus ou affiliés.

ARTICLE II.

Les Chevaliers d'Orient étant Souverains Princes de la Maçonnerie, pour en perpétuer la souveraineté, et y faire régner à jamais la bonne harmonie, seront tous égaux. C'est pourquoi la place eminente de Souverain sera rempli alternativement par tous les FF∴ d'année en année, chacun à leur tour.

ARTICLE III.

Il n'en sera pas de même du Grand Garde des Sceaux. Il sera perpétuel, attendu qu'il est le seul Grand Garde des Archives secrètes et anciennes de la Chevalerie, dépositaire des Sceaux, chargé de la correspondance générale dans toutes les Loges de ce grade répandues sur la surface de la terre. Il fera la convocation du Conseil, lorsqu'il en sera requis. Cette place sera donnée par élection à un Chevalier domicilié et habitué dans le lieu ou sera établie cette Grande Loge.

Lorsque cette place sera vacante, l'élection sera faite aussitôt entre les Chevaliers, à la pluralité des voix, par le scrutin. Il sera toujours placé le premier à droite du Souverain, et les visiteurs après lui.

ARTICLE IV.

La place de Général sera rempli alternativement par tous les Chevaliers, conformément à l'article 2. Ses fonctions sont de faire observer les règles et l'ordre.

STATUTES AND GENERAL REGULATIONS

Knights of the East.

ARTICLE I.

A Council of Knights of the East is composed of the Sovereign, the Grand Keeper of the Seals, the General, the Grand Treasurer, the Grand Orator or Minister of State, and all the Bro.·. Knights, received or affiliated.

ARTICLE II.

The Knights of the East, being Sovereign Princes of Masonry, must all be equal, in order to perpetuate their sovereignty, and make harmony always prevail. For that reason, the eminent post of Sovereign is to be filled alternately by all the Brethren from year to year, each in his turn.

ARTICLE III.

But it is not so with the office of Grand Keeper of the Seals. That officer holds in perpetuity, in consequence of his being the sole Grand Keeper of the Secret and Ancient Archives of Chivalry, the depositary of the Seals, and charged with the general correspondence with all bodies of this degree spread over the surface of the Earth. He convokes the Council when ordered to do so. This office is given by election to a Knight who is domiciled and resident in the place where this Grand Lodge is established.

When this office is vacant, an election to fill it is immediately held by the Knights, by ballot, and a plurality of votes elects. The incumbent always sits nearest the Sovereign, on his right, and next to him the Visitors.

ARTICLE IV.

The office of General is filled by all the Knights alternately, according to Art. 2. The duties of this officer are to see the rules and order observed.

ARTICLE V.

Le Grand Trésorier veillera de même à l'exécution des règlemens, et sera placé à gauche du Général, à l'Occident. Il sera dépositaire de tous les fonds et ornemens de la Loge. Il en rendra compte trois fois l'année à tous les FF∴ Chevaliers assemblés. On ne parviendra pas à cette place par ancienneté : il en sera nommé un tous les ans au scrutin, et s'il est favorable au même, il sera continué.

ARTICLE VI.

La place de Grand Orateur sera remplie par tous les Chevaliers alternativement, conformément aux articles 2 et 4. Il sera placé le premier à gauche du Souverain. Cependant, comme le talent de la parole est un don de la nature et rare, les Chevaliers auront la liberté de refuser cette place, sans être dans le cas de reproche.

ARTICLE VII.

De même que les Élus, Parfaits et Sublimes Maçons sont tous Grands Surveillans nés de l'Ordre de la Maçonnerie, les Chevaliers d'Orient sont les Princes et Souverains nés de l'Ordre en général. Le Conseil d'Orient connoîtra tous les différens qui naîtront parmi les Grands, Élus, Parfaits et Sublimes Maçons.

ARTICLE VIII.

Un Chevalier d'Orient a droit partout où il voyage, lorsqu'il rencontre un Maçon Apprentif, Compagnon ou Maître, pourvu qu'il n'y ait point de Loges des six derniers grades, établies dans le lieu où il se trouvera, de leur conférer ces six grades, mais en différens temps, s'il les en juge dignes ; quoique les Chevaliers aient le pouvoir d'en constituer d'autres, il ne le font cependant que dans des cas extraordinaires et qu'en faveur d'un frère qui ne serait pas domicilié dans une ville où résideroient des Chevaliers de ce grade, ne devant pas être trop multiplié, ou dans des lieux où il n'y auroit que des Loges établies sur de faux principes, ou avec de fausses constitutions ; en ce cas il a le droit de les interdire, ou de les mettre dans la bonne voie, selon sa sagesse et sa prudence.

ARTICLE IX.

Si un Chevalier a commis quelques fautes graves, on ne pourra lui infliger de peines, qu'après l'avoir entendu, et en avoir délibéré,

ARTICLE V.

The Grand Treasurer also sees to the enforcement of the Regulations, and sits on the left of the general, in the West. He is the custodian of all the funds and insignia of the Lodge. He renders his accounts three times a year to all the Knights assembled. This office is not filled by promotion; but by annual election by ballot, and the incumbent may be reëlected.

ARTICLE VI.

The office of Grand Orator is filled by all the Knights in turn, according to Articles 2 and 4. He sits on the left of the Sovereign. But, as talent and eloquence are rare gifts of Nature, a Knight may refuse to accept this office, without for that being liable to censure.

ARTICLE VII.

As all Elect, Perfect and Sublime Masons are ex-officio Wardens of the Order of Masonry, so Knights of the East are ex-officio Princes and Sovereigns of the Order in general. The Council of Knights of the East takes cognizance of all disagreements among Grand, Elect, Perfect and Sublime Masons.

ARTICLE VIII.

A Knight of the East has the right, wherever he travels, when he meets an Apprentice, Fellow Craft or Master Mason, provided there are in the place no Lodges of the six lower degrees, to confer on such Bro∴ those six degrees, if he find him worthy, but each at a different time. Though a Knight has the power to constitute other Knights, he does not do so except in extraordinary cases, and in favour of a Bro∴ domiciled in a place where no Knights of this degree reside; because it ought not to be too much multiplied; or in places where there are no Lodges except such as are established on false principles, or with irregular constitutions. In that case, he may either interdict such Lodges, or heal them, as his wisdom and prudence may direct.

ARTICLE IX.

If a Knight commit any grave offence, he is not to be punished therefor until he has been heard in his defence, nor until the matter

la Loge régulièrement assemblée à cet effet, c'est-à-dire qu'il faut que tous les Chevaliers d'Orient soient convoqués et que le plus grand nombre y soit. Les fautes et les punitions des Chevaliers seront tenues cachées aux frères des grades inférieurs, sous les plus grands peines. Les Conseils pour délibérer sur la police seront composés de sept Chevaliers au moins.

ARTICLE X.

Lorsqu'il sera question de faire passer un Élu, Parfait et Sublime Maçon au grade de Chevalier d'Orient, il sera proposé un mois avant, pour avoir le temps de s'informer s'il s'est acquitté de ses devoirs avec zèle et exactitude.

ARTICLE XI.

Tout Chevalier d'Orient a droit de commettre des Grands, Élus, Parfaits pour veiller à la conduite des FF.˙. qui aspirent aux Hauts Grades.

ARTICLE XII.

Nul Grand, Élu, Parfait ne pourra parvenir au grade de Chevalier d'Orient qu'il n'ait été nommé pour veiller à la conduite de tous les FF.˙., et qu'il ne s'en soit acquitté au moins pendant sept mois; le temps peut cependant être diminué, selon les circonstances.

ARTICLE XIII.

Quoiqu'il soit porté par les articles 2, 4 et 6, que les Chevaliers ne pourront exercer leurs offices que pendant un an, ils pourront cependant continuer une seconde année, s'il ne se trouve aucun Chevalier propre à remplir la place vacante. Le Jour de la Fête annuelle du 22 Mars, celui qui doit en sortir sera engagé à continuer une seconde année, pour le bien de l'Ordre.

ARTICLE XIV.

Tous les Chevaliers d'Orient doivent se mettre en état de remplir les places du grade des Souverains de l'Ordre de la Maçonnerie. Ils doivent être instruits que c'est pour cette raison, et par les principes d'égalité et d'harmonie qui doivent régner entr'eux, que les dignités doivent être possédées chacune tour à tour. En consé-

has been regularly tried, by the Lodge, met for that purpose; that is to say, when all the Knights of the East have been summoned to attend, and a majority of them is present. The offences committed by Knights, and the punishment inflicted, are to be kept from the knowledge of all Brethren of inferior degrees, under the greatest penalties. Councils held to consider matters of police must consist of seven Knights, at least.

ARTICLE X.

When it is desired to advance a Grand, Elect, Perfect and Sublime Mason to the degree of Knight of the East, a month, at least, must elapse after he is proposed, that the Council may have time to inform itself whether he has zealously and accurately performed his duties.

ARTICLE XI.

Every Knight of the East has the right to commission Grand, Elect, Perfect and Sublime Masons to supervise the conduct of such Brethren as aspire to the High Degrees.

ARTICLE XII.

No Grand, Elect, Perfect and Sublime Mason can attain the degree of Knight of the East, until he has been appointed to supervise the conduct of his Brethren, and has done so for seven months; but that time may be shortened according to circumstances.

ARTICLE XIII.

Although it is provided by Articles 2, 4 and 6, that a Knight holds office only one year, he may yet serve a second term, if no Knight be found, suitable to fill the vacant place. On the annual Feast-day of the 22d of March, he who should go out of office may in such case, and for the good of the Order, be required to serve a second term.

ARTICLE XIV.

All Knights of the East ought to qualify to fill the places of the Degree of Sovereigns of the Masonic Order. They should learn that it is for this reason, and upon those principles of harmony and equality that ought to govern among them, that the high offices are to be filled by each in his turn. Consequently, the Grand

quence, le Grand Conseil d'Orient s'assemblera une fois par mois, pour que les Chevaliers s'exercent alternativement sur tous les grades. Il seroit humiliant pour un Maçon, parvenu à la sublimité de ce grade, d'ignorer la science des grades inférieurs, lui qui est obligé d'instruire les autres.

ARTICLE XV.

Quand un Chevalier d'Orient visite une Loge de Perfection ou de Royal Arche, il doit être reçu avec les honneurs de la voûte; et si le Vénérable n'est point Chevalier, il est obligé de lui offrir le maillet et son siége, qu'il peut accepter ou refuser. S'il accepte, ce n'est que pour un moment; il s'assied à la droite du Vénérable, qui lui offre l'inspection de tous les travaux de la Loge. Si plusieurs Chevaliers visitent la Loge ensemble, ils prennent place à la droite et à la gauche du trois-fois-Puissant, qui offre le maillet au plus ancien.

ARTICLE XVI.

Chaque Chevalier aura une copie des présents articles, collationnée et certifiée véritable par le Grand Garde des Sceaux, une copie des Statuts et Règlemens de la Perfection, et une copie des Règlemens Généraux de la Loge du Premier Grade, afin d'être en état de maintenir le bon ordre et la discipline partout et dans toutes les Loges régulières qu'il visitera.

CHEVALIER COLLATIONNÉ et certifié véritable, par nous, Souverain Grand Commandeur et Grand Garde des Sceaux, du Grand Conseil du Royal Secret, à l'Orient de Charleston, Caroline du Sud.

[Signé par DELAHOGUE et DE GRASSE, comme les autres pièces.]

La copie d'AVEILHÉ certifié et visé comme les autres pièces, sous tous les rapports.

Council of the East will meet once a month for practice by each of the Knights alternately in all the degrees. It would be a humiliating thing for a Mason who has attained the sublime height of this degree, not to know the science of the inferior degrees, when he is obliged to instruct others therein.

ARTICLE XV.

When a Knight of the East visits a Lodge of Perfection or of the Royal Arch, he is to be received with the honours of the Vault; and if the Venerable is not a Knight, he must offer such visitor his mallet and his seat, which he may accept or refuse. If he accepts, he retains them but a moment, and then seats himself on the right of the Ven.·., who requests him to inspect all the work of the Lodge. If several Knights together visit a Lodge, they sit on the right and left of the Th.·. Puissant, who offers the mallet to the eldest.

ARTICLE XVI.

Every Knight must have a copy of these present articles, compared and certified to be correct by the Grand Keeper of the Seals, a copy of the Statutes and Regulations of Perfection, and a copy of the General Regulations for Lodges of the first degree, that he may be competent to maintain good order and discipline every where, and in all regular Lodges that he may visit.

COMPARED, and certified as correct by us, Sovereign Gr.·. Commander and Grand Keeper of the Seals of the Grand Council of the Royal Secret at the Orient of Charleston, South Carolina.

[Signed by DELAHOGUE and DE GRASSE, like the other documents.]

The copy of AVEILHÉ certified and *viséd* like the last document, in all respects.

[The following INSTITUTES, STATUTES and REGULATIONS are translated from the *Recueil des Actes du Suprême Conseil de France;* where they are given as a part or sequence of the Constitution of 1762, without any indication of date or parentage. I have not succeeded in learning any thing in regard to 'ADINGTON, CHANCELLOR;' but as they seem to have emanated from the Orient of 17° 58' North Lat., I presume they came from Gaudaloupe.]

INSTITUTES.

ART. 1. The Grand Inspectors General of the Order, and Presidents of the Sublime Councils of Princes of High Masonry, are by imprescriptible title the Chiefs of High Masonry.

ART. 2. The Tribunal that directs the administration of High Masonry, and constitutes the different dependent degrees thereof, is style the GRAND CONSISTORY.

ART. 3. The Grand Inspectors General, and the Presidents of the Grand Councils of the Sublime Princes of the Royal Secret, are life-members of the Grand Consistory.

ART. 4. The Grand Consistory is composed of the Grand Inspector of the Order, of the Presidents of the Councils of the Sublime Princes, and of twenty-one of the oldest of the Sublime Princes, taken in the order of priority of reception as such.

ART. 5. All Sublime Princes of the Royal Secret are entitled to be present in the assemblies of the Grand Consistory, and to partake of its deliberations.

ART. 6. To the Grand Consistory belongs all power in regard to the *doctrine of* High Masonry.

ART. 7. Twelve grand officers, selected out of the Grand Inspectors General, the Presidents of the Councils of the Sublime Princes, and those Sublime Princes who are members of the Grand Consistory, compose the Corps of Dignitaries of that body ; to wit :

> 1st. THE SOVEREIGN GRAND COMMANDER ;
> 2d. THE LIEUTENANT GRAND COMMANDER ;
> 3d. THE SECOND LIEUTENANT GRAND COMMANDER ;
> 4th. THE MINISTER OF STATE ;
> 5th. THE GRAND CHANCELLOR ;

6th. The Treasurer General;
7th. The Grand Keeper of the Seals and Archives;
8th. The Grand Master of Ceremonies.
9th. The Grand Expert Introducer;
10th. The Grand Expert Standard-bearer;
11th. The Grand Captain of the Guards;
12th. The Grand Hospitaller.

Art. 8. Every Grand Council of Sublime Princes of the Royal Secret, and every Council of Grand Elect Kadosch is entitled to be represented in the Grand Consistory by a Deputy, who must be selected from among the Sublime Princes duly patented and recognized.

Art. 9. The Sovereign Grand Commander, or in his place and by his authorization, the First Lieutenant Grand Commander, or in his absence the Second Lieutenant Grand Commander, are the only persons who can convoke and preside over the Grand Consistory: and if the special case should occur that all these three Grand officers are out of the jurisdiction, then, and always by special authorization, some one of the Grand officers shall be appointed in their stead, the nomination being made in a meeting of the Grand Consistory, specially convoked.

Art. 10. In a meeting of the Grand Consistory, specially convoked, seven members, including the Grand Commander or one of his Lieutenants, may open the work, and the proceedings will be legal, but under no pretext can any business be done with a less number.

STATUTES.

Art. 1. The Grand Consistory will meet four times a year, in Assembly of Communication,—on the 21st of March, 25th of June, 21st of September, and 27th of December. In these Communications whatever concerns High Masonry in general will be considered. Besides these four communications, one will be convoked every month, to give special consideration to the affairs of the Order.

Art. 2. Every three years, on the 27th of December, the Grand Consistory will elect its Grand Officers, from among the Grand

Inspectors General, the Presidents of the Councils of the Sublime Princes, and the twenty-one active members of the Grand Consistory. Those holding the Grand Offices may be reëlected.

ART. 3. The ex-Grand Officers of the Grand Consistory are entitled to a patent of the official rank which they have respectively held, wherein the time during which they held such office shall be specified.

ART. 4. There shall be appointed by the Grand Consistory, from among the Sublime Princes, Deputy Inspectors General, to represent it in the different places under its jurisdiction; whose powers shall be defined by the instructions given them, when their Constitutional patents shall be transmitted or delivered to them.

ART. 5. Each Deputy Inspector General shall, within his department, see executed the Institutes, Statutes and General Regulations of High Masonry, shall compel regularity in the work, and shall represent the Grand Consistory in whatever appertains to the General Administration, shall act as an Inspector, and shall make full report to the Grand Consistory, which report shall be read in the Grand Assemblies of Communication.

ART. 6. All questions brought before the Grand Consistory shall be settled and determined by plurality of votes. The President alone shall have two votes. No question can be discussed except on a motion seconded, nor any one decided until the opinion of the Minister of State has been given.

ART. 7. The resolutions of the Grand Councils of the Sublime Princes, when an appeal is taken therefrom to the Grand Consistory, shall not have execution until after affirmance by the Grand Consistory, and notification of the resolution of affirmance.

ART. 8. There shall be appointed, in the bosom of the Grand Consistory, a Committee of General Administration, composed of six members, including always the Minister of State, the Grand Chancellor and the Treasurer General. This Committee shall be required to furnish reports of its action and decisions, but these shall be provisionally executed in cases of emergency.

ART. 9. A register shall be kept, of all the Sublime Princes of the Royal Secret, who are duly recognized and patented, containing the date of reception of each, his name, surname, age and domicil.

ART. 10. Each Grand Council of Sublime Princes of the Royal Secret, Council of Knights Kadosch, &c., &c., shall keep a register;

containing the dates of their Patents of Constitution, the circumstances of their establishment, and the names of their members; all in accordance with the reports made by the different Deputy Inspectors General.

ART. 11. The Grand Keeper of the Seals shall affix the seal only upon the signature of the Sovereign Grand Commander, or his Representative; in matters affecting the General Administration, only upon those of the Minister of State and Grand Chancellor: and to Patents to be issued, only on those of the seven first Grand Officers.

ART. 12. All petitions presented to the Grand Consistory, for Patents of Constitution to establish a Sacred Asylum of High Masonry, shall be referred to the Inspector General of the Department, who shall annex thereto his report showing the Masonic character of the petitioners, and his opinion as to the propriety of refusing or granting the Patent, with an exact statement of the names, surnames, ages, occupations and domicils of the Petitioners, that upon full advice the Grand Consistory may determine as may seem right.

ART. 13. The Grand Inspectors General of the Order, duly patented and recognized, in foreign countries where there is no Grand Consistory, have the incontestable right to erect, constitute, prohibit, suspend and exclude, in the Lodges of Perfection, &c., as they shall deem proper; they reporting to the Grand Consistory from which their powers are derived; and on the express charge of conforming strictly to the Institutes, Statutes and General Regulations of High Masonry.

ART. 14. A Patent of Constitution for the establishment of a Sacred Asylum of High Masonry shall not issue, unless there be at least five Brethren to compose it, of the degree of Sublime Princes of the Royal Secret, for a Sovereign Grand Council of that degree; seven Knights Elect Kadosch for a Grand Council of that degree; and seven of the proper degree for any other body.

ART. 15. A register shall be kept, divided into four columns; the first of which shall contain the petitions presented by the different Lodges of Perfection or by the Deputy Inspectors General; the second, the name of the Department, the locality of the body, and the vertical point; the third, the names of the Commissioners who report on the application; and the fourth, the decisions thereon. The Chancellor General shall alone have the right to make extracts from this Register, and deliver him to those entitled to receive

7

them, compared and signed by them, and sealed with the Great Seal.

ART. 16. At the time of the installation of a Sacred Asylum of High Masonry, the members composing it shall all make and sign their pledge of obedience to the Institutes, Statutes and General Regulations of High Masonry : a duplicate whereof shall be sent up by the Deputy Inspector General to the Grand Consistory, to be deposited in the archives, with the other proceedings at such installation.

ART. 17. The form of the pledge shall be as follows :

" We, the undersigned, ... do hereby declare that we do agree to abide by and execute the Institutes, Statutes, and General Regulations, and obey the Supreme Tribunal of High Masonry, conformably to the tenor and true meaning of the obligations which we have assumed in the initiations into the several Sublime degrees that we have received."

ART. 18. The installation of a Sacred Asylum of High Masonry in the Capital or Seat of the Grand Consistory, shall be always done by three of its members; and in a Province, by the Deputy Inspector General of the jurisdiction, who, in such case, is authorized to delegate part of his powers to the two highest in degree among the brethren, that they may assist him in the installation.

IN the fullness of their wisdom and power, the Chiefs and true Protectors of High Masonry have decreed and established the present Institutes, Statutes and General Regulations, to be at all points kept and observed according to their form and tenor.

GIVEN at the Central point of the True Light, the 20th day of the 2d Month, Ijar, of the year of the world 5732.

 (*Compared and signed*)   ADINGTON,

           Grand Chancellor.

TO THE GLORY OF THE GRAND ARCHITECT OF THE UNIVERSE!

Lux ex Tenebris!

AT the Orient of the world, under the C∴ C∴ of the Zenith, near the Burning Bush, at the vertical point that answers to 17° 58′ South [North?] Lat.∴, under the sign of Capricorn, of the 9th day of the 2d Month named Ijar, 5801.

By order of the Grand Sovereign Consistory of Princes Metropolitan of Heredom, I, the Grand Chancellor, have delivered and certified the following extract from the General Collection of Contitutional Balustres of the Grand Metropolitan Consistory, to be transmitted to the Grand Deputy of the Grand Consistory established at the Central point of 18° 47′ North Latitude.

(*Signed*) ADINGTON,

Grand Chancellor.

EXTRACT

FROM THE

COLLECTION OF CONSTITUTIONAL BALUSTRES.

Instructions as to the General Principles

OF

High Masonry.

ART. 1. Whenever, in a State where there is neither a Grand Consistory nor a Grand Council of Sublime Princes of the Royal Secret, there are any Grand Inspectors General and Princes of the Royal Secret, the Grand Inspector General whose patent and recognition bear the oldest date, or, if there be no Inspectors Gen-

eral, then the oldest Prince of the Royal Secret, is invested with the administrative and dogmatic power of High Masonry, and takes accordingly the title of Sovereign.

ART. 2. He confers the last degrees, and gives patents thereupon, without other formality than the counter-signature of his Grand Chancellor.

ART. 3. In cases not provided for by the law of High Masonry, his decisions have the force of law, and are to be executed throughout his jurisdiction.

ART. 4. The Grand Inspectors-General, and Princes of the Royal Secret, have the right to initiate, to inspect Masonic work, and to exercise a general superintendence over the execution of the Institutes, Statutes, and General Regulations; but, in all cases, they must report their action to the Sovereign, and it must be sanctioned and *viséd* by him.

ART. 5. Every Grand Inspector General, or Prince of the Royal Secret, in the cases provided for by articles 1, 2 and 3, must keep an exact record of his masonic action, each act in the regular order of its date.

ART. 6. This record should be opened by an entry stating the masonic character of the person keeping it, the purpose of the Register, and the names and quality of those whom he initiates, and be closed by a *ne varietur paraphèd*, with mention of the number of folios of which the Register consists.

ART. 7. Whenever a Grand Inspector General, or Prince of the Royal Secret, recognizes a brother of the same rank, he should *visé* the patent of such brother, and have his own *viséd* by him, the *visa* being dated, and giving the vertical point of the place.

ART. 8. Every Grand Inspector or Prince of the Royal Secret must require all whom he initiates or affiliates, before their reception, to take the obligation prescribed by the General Regulations of High Masonry; and he is required to dismiss those who refuse to comply with this pre-requisite.

ART. 9. A Grand Inspector General, or Prince of the Royal Secret must take the greatest care to enter upon his register every Masonic act done by him, in the order in which, and as soon as, each is done, and accurately to index it, so that every entry may be readily referred to; and he must also have each entry signed by the person affiliated, initiated, &c.; as also a duplicate of the necessary obligation, to be laid up in his archives.

ART. 10. Those Grand Inspectors General and Princes Masons who are at too great a distance to obtain the sanction and *visa* of the Sovereign, must at least once a year forward to him a copy of the minutes of their proceedings, in due form, to obtain his sanction.

ART. 11. In a Country where there is no Grand Consistory established, but only Grand Councils of the Sublime Princes Masons of the Royal Secret, the Grand Inspectors General and Princes Masons can exercise their powers only when domiciled at least 25 leagues from the nearest Council.

ART. 12. As soon as a Grand Consistory is established in a Country, the Grand Inspectors General and Princes Masons lose the right of individually exercising the administrative and doctrinal power, it being then concentered in the Central Authority.

ART. 13. The Grand Inspectors General and Princes Masons, when seven of them meet in General Committee, in a country where no Legislative Body of High Masonry exists, may apply for a charter of organization to the Sovereign Grand Inspector General; who has, in that case, authority to constitute the body applied for.

Of Legislation.

ONLY CHAPTER.

The Grand Dignitaries of at least five Grand Councils of Sublime Princes, met in General Committee in the Metropolis of a Country in which no Legislative Body of High Masonry has been established, have the right to organize a Constituent Chapter General, and to select from the members of the Committee those who shall compose it; conforming in all respects to the laws of High masonry.

Of Administration and Doctrine.

ART. 1. The Grand Inspectors General and Princes of the Royal Secret, met in General Committee in the Metropolis of a country where no Consistory is yet established, have the right to organize themselves into a Grand Consistory, and to select from the members of the Committee those who are to compose the Consistory; conforming, in establishing the same, to the general laws of High Masonry.

ART. 2. All the Grand Inspectors General and Princes Masons throughout such country should be convoked on the occasion ; and to be recognized as such, each should be legally patented, and his patent regularly sealed, signed and counter-signed.

ART. 3. The Consistory so established will be at once invested with all the administrative and doctrinal power allowed by the laws of High Masonry.

Of the Organization of the Grand Consistory.

ART. 1. The Grand Consistory is organized as follows :

Twelve Grand Officers or Dignitaries are chosen at will from among the Grand Inspectors General and the Presidents of the Grand Councils of the Sublime Princes, who are members by right of the Grand Consistory, and from among the twenty-one eldest Princes Masons, duly patented and recognized.

ART. 2. After the Grand Dignitaries of the Consistory are elected, a Supreme Council of Grand Inspectors General, or Grand Council of Appeal and Legislation is established.

ART. 3. The twelve eldest Grand Inspectors General, not being Grand Dignitaries, form the Grand Council of Appeal ; in which character they take the oath and are proclaimed.

ART. 4. In the deliberations of the Grand Consistory, the members of the Grand Council of Appeal may join in debate, but do not vote.

ART. 5. In case there should not be a sufficient number of Grand Inspectors General to complete the Grand Consistory, the eldest Presidents of the Councils, and in default of them, the eldest of the Princes Members of the Councils, are proclaimed Grand Inspectors General, and members of the Grand Consistory.

ART. 6. Besides the twenty-one active members, there are selected, always in the order of their age, from among the Sublime Princes, adjunct members, to complete the number of the Grand Consistory, which is fixed at eighty-one : so that the Grand Dignitaries, Grand Officers, Members of the Supreme Grand Council of Appeal, Presidents of the Councils, and the active and adjunct members, to the number in all of eighty-one, complete the Grand Consistory.

ART. 7. The Adjunct Members, though a part of the Grand Consistory, have only a consultative voice therein ; but they may be

called to fill temporarily the places and perform the duties of the Dignitaries and Officers.

ART. 8. They of right take the place of the active members in the deliberations; in which case they have a right to vote, and succeed to all the rights of those whose places they fill.

ART. 9. The Deputies or Representatives of the Sublime Councils of Princes can be selected from among them only.

ART. 10. They may be appointed to serve on Committees and as members of Deputations, and to perform other duties in the ceremonial of the Grand Consistory.

Of the Prerogatives of the Grand Councils of the Sublime Princes of the Royal Secret.

ART. 1. The Grand Councils of Princes Masons exercise the Departmental power in their respective jurisdictions.

ART. 2. They have the power of inspection of all the works of High Masonry.

ART. 3. And of seeing to the execution of the general laws of High Masonry, and the particular regulations of the Grand Consistory.

ART. 4. They transmit and present directly to the Grand Consistory, in their own names, the petitions for patents and charters preferred to them by the Chapters and Councils under their jurisdiction.

Of the Deputy Inspectors General.

ART. 1. The Deputy Inspectors General established in jurisdictions where there is no Grand Consistory, will be the representatives of the Grand Consistory, and perform those duties of supervision and inspection that are above assigned to the Grand Councils of the Sublime Princes.

ART. 2. They are, however, bound in all respects to conform to what is prescribed for their government by the laws of High Masonry.

EXEMPLIFICATION *compared and certified to be correct:*

[*Signed.*]   ADINGTON,
                                        Grand Chancellor.

AD UNIVERSI TERRARUM ORBIS SUMMI ARCHITECTI GLORIAM.

VERA INSTITUTA SECRETA ET FUNDAMENTA

ORDINIS

VETERUM-STRUCTORUM-LIBERORUM-AGGREGATORUM

ATQUE

CONSTITUTIONES MAGNÆ

ANTIQUI-ACCEPTI-RITUS-SCOTICI,

ANNI MDCCLXXXVI

EVULGATA AUSPICIIS SUPREMI CONCILII PRO JURISDICTIONE
MERIDIANA CIVITATUM FŒDERATARUM AMERICÆ.

ANNO MDCCCLIX.

AD UNIVERSI TERRARUM ORBIS SUMMI ARCHITECTI GLORIAM.

VÉRITABLES INSTITUTS SECRETS ET BASES FONDAMENTALES

DE

L'ORDRE

DES ANCIENS FRANCS-MAÇONS-UNIS

ET

GRANDES CONSTITUTIONS

DU RITE ANCIEN-ACCEPTÉ-ÉCOSSAIS,

DE L'AN 1786.

PUBLIÉS SOUS LES AUSPICES DU SUPREME CONSEIL POUR LA JURIDICTION MÉRIDIONALE
DES ETATS UNIS D'AMÉRIQUE.

TRADUIT DU LATIN

PAR

L'ILL.·. F.·. CHARLES LAFFON DE LADÉBAT, 33e.

1859.

AD UNIVERSI TERRARUM ORBIS SUMMI ARCHITECTI GLORIAM.

THE TRUE SECRET INSTITUTES AND BASES

OF

THE ORDER

OF ANCIENT FREE AND ASSOCIATED MASONS,

AND

THE GRAND CONSTITUTIONS

OF THE ANCIENT-ACCEPTED-SCOTTISH RITE,

OF THE YEAR 1786.

PUBLISHED BY AUTHORITY OF THE SUPREME COUNCIL FOR THE SOUTHERN
JURISDICTION OF THE UNITED STATES OF AMERICA.

TRANSLATED FROM THE LATIN

BY

ILL∴ BRO∴ ALBERT PIKE, 33d.

1859.

Grand Constitutions of 1786.

NOVA INSTITUTA SECRETA

ET FUNDAMENTA,

ANTIQUISSIMÆ, VENERANDISSIMÆQUE SOCIETATIS VETERUM-STRUC-
TORUM-LIBERORUM-AGGREGATORUM, QUÆ REGIUS AC MILITARIS
LIBERÆ-ARTIS-FABRICÆ-LAPIDARIÆ ORDO VOCATUR.

Nos, FREDERICUS, *Dei gratiâ, Rex Borussiæ, Margravius Bran-*
deburgi, etc., etc., etc.:
Supremus Magnus Protector, Magnus Commendator, Magnus
Magister Universalis, et Conservator antiquissimæ et venerabilis
Societatis Veterum-Liberorum-Aggregatorum-Structorum vel La-

NOUVEAUX INSTITUTS SECRETS

ET BASES FONDAMENTALES

DE LA TRÈS ANCIENNE ET TRÈS RESPECTABLE SOCIÉTÉ DES ANCIENS
FRANCS-MAÇONS UNIS, CONNUE SOUS LE NOM D'ORDRE ROYAL
ET MILITAIRE DE L'ART LIBRE DE TAILLER LA PIERRE.

Nous, FRÉDÉRIC, *par la grâce de Dieu, Roi de Prusse, Mar-*
grave de Brandebourg, etc., etc., etc.:
Souverain Grand Protecteur, Grand Commandeur, Grand
Maître Universel et Conservateur de la très ancienne et très respec-
table Société des Anciens Francs-Maçons ou Architectes unis, au-
trement appelée l'ORDRE Royal et Militaire de l'Art Libre de
Tailler la Pierre ou Franche-Maçonnerie:

A TOUS LES ILLUSTRES ET BIEN-AIMES FRERES
QUI CES PRESENTES VERRONT:

Tolerance, Union, Prosperite.

Il est évident et incontestable que, fidèle aux importantes
obligations que nous nous sommes imposées en acceptant le
protectorat de la très ancienne et très respectable Institution
connue de nos jours sous le nom de " *Société de l'Art Libre de*
tailler la Pierre " ou " ORDRE DES ANCIENS FRANCS MAÇONS UNIS "

*tomorum seu Regalis et Militaris ORDINIS Liberæ-Artis-Fabri-
cæ Lapidariæ vel Liberæ-Latomiæ:*

ILLUSTRIBUS ET DILECTIS FRATRIBUS PRÆSENTES INSPECTURIS:

Tolerantiam, Unionem, Prosperitatem.

Quod compertum et exploratum ipsi Nos habemus, conservantia
et summa Officia quæ pacti sumus cum antiquissimâ reverendissimâ-
que Institutione notâ ævo nostro, sub nomine *Liberæ-Artis-Fabricæ-
Lapidariæ-Fraternitatis* aut ORDINIS VETERUM-STRUCTORUM-LIBE-

---

THE NEW SECRET INSTITUTES
AND BASES

OF THE MOST ANCIENT AND MOST WORSHIPFUL SOCIETY OF ANCIENT
AND ASSOCIATED FREE-MASONS, WHICH IS STYLED THE ROYAL AND
MILITARY ORDER OF THE FREE ART OF WORKING IN STONE.

We, FREDERIC, *by the grace of God, King of Prussia, Margrave
of Brandenburg, etc., etc.:*
*Supreme Grand Protector, Grand Commander, Universal
Grand Master, and Defender of the most ancient and honorable
Society of Ancient Free and Associated Masons or Builders, or of
the Royal and Military ORDER of the Free Art of Working in
Stone, or of Free-Masonry:*

TO ALL ILLUSTRIOUS AND BELOVED BRETHREN TO WHOM THESE PRESENTS SHALL COME:

Toleration, Union, Prosperity.

We hold it to be certain and undeniable, that the high duty of
protection which we have assumed towards that most ancient and
worshipful Institution, known in this age as *the Fraternity of the
Free Art of Working in Stone,* or THE ORDER OF FREE AND ASSO-

8

RORUM-AGGREGATORUM, fecerunt, quod notum est omnibus, ut illam
nostrâ speciali sollicitudine tutaremur.

Hæc universalis Institutio, quæ originem à societatis humanæ
origine ducit, est pura in dogmate et doctrinâ, sapiens, prudens et
moralis in disciplinis, exercitationibus, consiliis ac rationibus, et fine
insigniter philosophico, sociali et humano se præsertim commendat;
hujusce societatis finis hic est: Concordia, Felicitas, Progressus,
Commoda humani generis generatim sumpti, et particulariter unius-
cujusque hominis: igitur omni spe et operâ, constanti animo uti
debet, ut ad eum exitum, quem solum se dignum profitetur, perveniat.

Sed, progrediente ætate, organorum compositio priscique regiminis unitas graviter adulteratæ sunt magnis eversionibus rerumque

---

nous nous sommes appliqué, comme chacun sait, à l'entourer de
notre sollicitude particulière.

Cette Institution universelle, dont l'origine remonte au berceau
de la société humaine, est pure dans son Dogme et sa Doctrine :
elle est sage, prudente et morale dans ses enseignements, sa pra-
tique, ses desseins et ses moyens : elle se recommande surtout par son
but philosophique, social et humanitaire. Cette société a pour objet l'U-
nion, le Bonheur, le Progrès et le Bien-Etre de la famille humaine en
général et de chaque homme individuellement. Elle doit donc travailler avec confiance et énergie et faire des efforts incessants pour
atteindre ce but, le seul qu'elle reconnaisse comme digne d'elle.

Mais, dans la suite des temps, la composition des organes de la
Maçonnerie et l'unité de son gouvernement primitif ont subi de
graves atteintes, causées par les grands bouleversements et les ré-
volutions qui, en changeant la face du monde ou en le soumettant à
des vicissitudes continuelles, ont, à différentes époques, soit dans
l'antiquité, soit de nos jours, dispersé les anciens Maçons sur toute
la surface du globe. Cette dispersion a donné naissance à des systèmes hétérogènes qui existent aujourd'hui sous le nom de RITES
et dont l'ensemble compose l'ORDRE.

Cependant d'autres divisions, nées des premières, ont donné lieu
à l'organisation de nouvelles sociétés : la plupart de celles-ci n'ont
rien de commun avec l'*Art Libre de la Franche-Maçonnerie*,
sauf le nom et quelques formules conservées par les fondateurs,
pour mieux cacher leurs desseins secrets—desseins souvent trop ex-
clusifs, quelquefois dangereux et presque toujours contraires aux

mutationibus quæ mundi statum everterunt aut alternis vicibus immutârunt, et quæ priscos Structores, diversis antiquorum nostrûmque temporum periodis, in varias orbis partes sparserunt. Hic dispersus sejunctiones operatus est, quæ sub RITUUM nomine hodiè vigent et quorum conjunctio ORDINEM componit.

Sed divisiones aliæ primis ex divisionibus ortæ, novis societatibus constituendis locum dederunt, et plurimis nulla alia cum *Liberâ-Arte-Fabricæ-Lapidariæ* est communitas, præter nomen aliasque formulas à fundatoribus servatas ut tegerent consilia secreta, sæpè exclusoria, aliquandò etiam periculosa et ferè semper principiis doctrinisque sublimibus *Liberæ-Artis-Fabricæ-Lapidariæ*, traditione transmissis, opposita.

Notæ discordiæ novis illis societatibus in ORDINE concitatæ,

CIATED MASONS, has caused us, as is known to all men, to guard it with the most scrupulous care.

That universal institution, whose origin goes back to the origin of human society, is pure in dogma and doctrine; wise, prudent and moral in its teachings, its practice, its purposes and its measures; and especially commends itself by its philosophical, social and humane design. For that design is the Harmony, the Happiness, the Progress and the Well-being of the Human Family as a whole, and of every man as an individual: wherefore it should hopefully and with a constant resolution use every exertion to attain to that end, which alone it regards as worthy of itself.

But in the progress of time, the organic symmetry of Masonry, and the unity of its primitive regimen have been greatly departed from, by those great commotions and changes in human affairs, that have overturned the world, or disturbed it with constant change; and which, at different periods, in ancient times and in our own, have dispersed the ancient Masons over all the earth. This dispersion has produced systems varying from each other, which still exist and are styled RITES; the aggregate whereof composes THE ORDER.

But still other divisions, springing from the first, caused the constitution of new associations, most of which have nothing whatever in common with the LIBERAL ART OF FREE-MASONRY, except the name and some forms preserved by their founders to keep secret their purposes,—purposes often exclusive, sometimes dangerous,

et per nimium tempus alitæ, illum suspicionibus et diffidentiæ omnium ferè Principum objecerunt, etiamque sævis nonnullorum in-
sectationibus.

Conatibus Structorum virtute præstantium sedatæ fuêre discordiæ, et illi omnes, jàm à longo tempore votis exposcunt, ut
generaliter in eas consulatur, rationibusque eos reditus impediant,
ORDINEMQUE sustineant, illi sui regiminis, organorumque
priscæ compositionis unitatem, priscamque disciplinam restitu-
endo.

Hæc vota accipiendo, quæ vota Nobis communia sunt à completâ
initiatione nostrâ mysteriis *Liberæ-Artis-Fabricæ-Lapidariæ*, Nobis
attamen dissimulare potuimus nec numerum, nec naturam, nec
veram magnitudinem obstaculorum removendorum ut illa vota per-

---

principes et aux sublimes doctrines de la *Franche-Maçonnerie*, tels
que nous les avons reçus de la tradition.

Les dissensions bien connues que ces nouvelles associations ont
suscitées dans l'ORDRE et qu'elles y ont trop longtemps fomen-
tées, ont éveillé les soupçons et la méfiance de presque tous les
Princes dont quelques-uns l'ont même persécuté cruellement.

Des Maçons, d'un mérite éminent, ont enfin réussi à appaiser ces
dissensions et tous ont, depuis longtemps, exprimé le désir qu'elles
fussent l'objet d'une délibération générale afin d'aviser aux moyens
d'en empêcher le retour et d'assurer le maintien de l'ORDRE, en
rétablissant l'unité dans son gouvernement et dans la composition
primitive de ses organes, ainsi que son antique discipline.

Tout en partageant ce désir que nous-même avons éprouvé
depuis le jour où nous avons été complètement initié aux mystères
de la *Franche-Maçonnerie*, nous n'avons pu, cependant, nous dissi-
muler ni le nombre, ni la nature, ni la grandeur réelle des obstacles
que nous aurions à surmonter pour accomplir ce désir. Notre premier soin a été de consulter les membres les plus sages et les plus
éminents de l'Ordre dans tous les pays sur les mesures les plus
convenables à adopter pour atteindre un but si utile, en respectant
les idées de chacun, sans faire violence à la juste indépendance des
Maçons et surtout à la liberté d'opinion qui est la première et la
plus sacrée de toutes les libertés et en même temps la plus prompte
à prendre ombrage.

Jusqu'à présent les devoirs qui nous étaient plus particulièrement
imposés comme Roi, les évènements nombreux et importants qui

solverentur. De tali re faciendâ rationem inire meditabamur deliberando, cum fratribus sapientissimis et principibus Fraternitatis in omnibus orbis regionibus, de consiliis aptissimis ad utilem illum exitum consequendum, violato nullius arbitrio, nullâ verâ Structorum libertate violatâ, nec opinionum præcipuè, quæ inter omnes libertates prima et sacerrima est atque admodùm propensa ad accepiendam offensionem.

Usquè adhuc Regis officia, nobis magis peculiaria, et plurimi gravesque eventus, qui nostri principatûs cursum insignierunt, irritam erga hoc fecerunt nostram voluntatem, et à proposito illo nos deterruerunt. Absolutio perfectioque tàm magni, pulchri, æqui ac necessarii operis, ad tempus, prudentiam, cognitionem studiumque fratrum, qui nobis succedent, deinceps pertinent: illud pensum illis

---

and almost always opposed to the traditional principles and sublime doctrines of *Free-Masonry*.

The well-known dissensions which those new associations excited and long kept alive in THE ORDER, exposed it to the suspicion and distrust of almost all monarchs, and to the cruel persecutions of some.

By the exertions of those Masons most eminent in virtue, these dissensions have been settled; and all have long and ardently desired that there should be a general consultation in regard thereto; and that the recurrence of like disorders should be prevented, and THE ORDER maintained, by restoring to it the unity of its original regimen, and of the pristine composition of its organs, as well as its ancient discipline.

While sharing these desires, which we have felt from the period when we were fully initiated into the mysteries of *Free-Masonry*, still we could not conceal from ourselves either the number, nature or true magnitude of the obstacles that must be removed before those desires can be fulfilled. We thought of taking the first step towards effecting the desired object, by taking counsel with the wisest and most eminent members of the Fraternity in every country, as to the measures most suitable to be adopted in order to attain the end desired, without doing violence to the wishes of any one, and in no wise interfering with that liberty that is the heritage of Masons, and especially the right of private judgment, which of all rights is first and most sacred, and most jealous of any encroachment.

relinquimus, præcipimusque ut sine intermissione, leniter ac prudenter dent illi operam.

Attamen recentes ac instantes expositiones quæ ad nos, his proximis temporibus, omnibus ex locis, missæ fuêre, nobis notam reddunt urgentem necessitatem opponendi potentem molem animo intolerantiæ, sectæ, schismatis et anarchiæ, quem inter fratres nuperi novatores adsciscere conantur, spectantes ad consilia plùs minùsve restricta, inconsiderata aut vituperabilia, et oblata sub speciosis rationibus quæ à proposito veram *Artem-Fabricæ-Lapidariæ*, naturam ejus immutando, deflectere, et sic ad contemptionem extinctionemque ORDINIS pervenire possunt. Confitemur Nosmetipsi hanc urgentem necessitatem, edocti omnia quæ in regnis vicinorum hodiè geruntur.

---

ont signalé notre règne ont paralysé nos bonnes intentions et nous ont détourné du but que nous nous étions proposé. C'est désormais au temps, ainsi qu'à la sagesse, à l'instruction et au zèle des frères qui viendront après nous qu'il appartiendra d'accomplir et de perfectionner une œuvre si grande et si belle, si juste et si nécessaire. C'est à eux que nous léguons cette tâche, et nous leur recommandons d'y travailler sans cesse, mais patiemment et avec précaution.

Toutefois, de nouvelles et pressantes représentations qui, de toutes parts, nous ont été adressées, dans ces derniers temps, nous ont convaincu de la nécessité d'opposer immédiatement une barrière puissante à l'esprit d'intolérance, de secte, de schisme et d'anarchie que des novateurs cherchent aujourd'hui à introduire parmi les frères. Leurs desseins ont plus ou moins de portée et sont ou imprudents, ou répréhensibles : présentés sous de fausses couleurs, ces desseins, en changeant la nature de l'*Art Libre de la Franche-Maçonnerie*, tendent à la détourner de son but, et doivent nécessairement causer la déconsidération et la ruine de l'ORDRE. En présence de tout ce qui se passe dans les royaumes voisins, nous reconnaissons qu'une intervention de notre part est devenue indispensable.

Ces raisons et *d'autres causes non moins graves* nous imposent donc le devoir d'assembler et de réunir en un seul corps de *Maçonnerie* tous les RITES du Régime ECOSSAIS dont les doctrines sont, de l'aveu de tous, à peu près les mêmes que celles des anciennes Institutions qui tendent au même but, et qui, n'étant que les branches principales d'un seul et même arbre, ne diffèrent entr'elles que par

Igitur hæ rationes *aliæque causæ non minoris ponderis* nos impellunt ad colligendum et agglomerandum in unum corpus *Artem-Fabricæ-Lapidariæ* omnes RITUS SCOTICI regiminis, quorum doctrinæ generaliter agnoscuntur esse maximè eædem ac illæ priscæ institutiones,quæ eòdem tendunt, et quæ, cùm sint præcipui rami ejusdem arboris, tantùm inter se differunt formulis, jàm inter multos explanatis, et quas conciliare facile est. Hi RITUS sunt qui agnoscuntur sub nomine *Antiqui, Heredom* aut *Hairdom, Kilwinning Orientis, Sancti-Andreæ, Imperatorum Orientis et Occidentis, Principum-Regii-Secreti* aut *Perfectionis, Philosophiæ,* et RITUS recentissimus, *Primævus* dictus.

IGITUR, acceptum habendo, pro basi nostræ reformationis conservatricis, titulum primi illorum Rituum et numerum graduum

---

Hitherto, the duties of the Regal office, that have in an especial manner weighed on us, and the very many and grave events that have marked the course of our reign, have made this our intention ineffectual, and deterred us from its performance. The completion and perfection of so great and beautiful, so just and necessary a work, must needs await the leisure, the wisdom, the knowledge and the zeal of the brethren who shall come after us. To them we bequeath the task, urging them to labour thereat unintermittedly, but slowly and with a prudent caution.

But recent and urgent representations, which of late have reached us from every quarter, have satisfied us of the urgent necessity of erecting a strong barrier against that spirit of intolerance, sectarianism, schism and anarchy, which late innovators are busily labouring to introduce among the brethren, aiming at objects more or less narrow, inconsiderate or reprehensible, and proposed for specious reasons, and which, by changing the nature of the true *Art of Free-Masonry*, necessarily tend to lead it astray, and may thus bring THE ORDER into general contempt and lead to its extinction. And we, advised of what is now passing in the neighbouring kingdoms, cannot but admit the existence of this urgent and pressing necessity.

Wherefore these reasons, *and other considerations of no less weight,* impel us to collect together and unite into one body and *Art of Masonry* all the RITES of the SCOTTISH regimen, the doctrines whereof are generally acknowledged to be in the main the same as those ancient institutions which tend to a common centre;

hierarchicum ultimi, DECLARAMUS illos omnes jàm nunc conjunctos et agglomeratos in unum solum ORDINEM qui, profitendo dogma et puras doctrinas priscæ *Artis-Fabricæ-Lapidariæ*, complectitur systemata omnia Scotici Ritûs copulata sub titulo RITUS-SCOTICI-ANTIQUI-ACCEPTI.

Doctrina largietur Structoribus in gradibus triginta tribus, in septem Templa aut classes partitis, quos quisque Structor vicissim lustrare tenebitur, antequàm ad sublimissimum ac ultimum perveniat; ac in quoque gradu, subibit moras et pericula quæ Instituta, Decreta Præscriptaque antiqua ac nova ORDINIS atque *Perfectionis* exigunt.

Primus gradus secundo subjicietur, iste tertio, et sic ex ordine usquè ad sublimem—tertium et trigesimum ac ultimum—qui ad om-

---

des formules, maintenant connues de plusieurs, et qu'il est facile de concilier. Ces RITES sont ceux connus sous les noms de Rite *Ancien*, *d'Hérédom* ou *d'Hairdom**, de *l'Orient de Kilwinning*, de *Saint-André*, des *Empereurs d'Orient et d'Occident*, des *Princes du Royal Secret* ou *de Perfection*, de Rite *Philosophique* et enfin de Rite *Primitif*, le plus récent de tous.

Adoptant, en conséquence, comme base de notre réforme salutaire, le titre du premier de ces Rites et le nombre des Degrés de la hiérarchie du dernier, nous les DÉCLARONS maintenant et à jamais réunis en un seul ORDRE qui, professant le Dogme et les pures Doctrines de l'antique *Franche-Maçonnerie*, embrasse tous les systèmes du Rite Ecossais sous le nom de RITE ÉCOSSAIS ANCIEN ACCEPTÉ.

La doctrine sera communiquée aux Maçons en trente-trois Degrés, divisés en sept Temples ou Classes. Tout Maçon sera tenu de parcourir successivement chacun de ces Degrés avant d'arriver au plus sublime et dernier ; et à chaque Degré, il devra subir tels délais et telles épreuves qui lui seront imposés conformément aux Instituts, Décrets et Règlemens anciens et nouveaux de l'ORDRE, ainsi qu'à ceux du Rite de *Perfection*.

Le premier Degré sera conféré avant le deuxième, celui-ci avant le troisième et ainsi de suite jusqu'au Degré Sublime—le trente-troisième et dernier—qui surveillera, dirigera et gouvernera tous les autres. Un Corps ou Réunion de membres possédant ce Degré

---

* Peut-être devrions-nous lire *Hæredum* et *Harodim*, au lieu de *Heredom* et *Hairdom* qui ne signifient rien.

nes alios advigilabit, illos redarguet, illisque imperabit, et cujus congregatio aut conventus, MAGNUM-CONCILIUM-SUPREMUM, dogmaticum erit, *Defensor, Conservatorque* ORDINIS, quem gubernabit atque administrabit, ex præsentibus et ex Constitutionibus quæ proximè instituentur.

Omnes gradus Rituum supra agglomeratorum, à primo ad octavum decimum, in gradibus Ritûs *Perfectionis,* ordini suo respondenti, et ex suâ analogiâ et similitudine, collocabuntur, et XVIII primos gradus RITUS-SCOTICI-ANTIQUI-ACCEPTI component. Undevigesimus gradus ac tertius et vigesimus gradus Ritûs, qui *Primævus* vocatur, vigesimus ORDINIS erit: vigesimus, ac tertius et vigesimus gradus *Perfectionis,* aut decimus sextus, ac quartus et vigesimus Ritûs *Primævi,* primus et vigesimus, ac octavus et vigesimus ORDINIS

---

and which, while only the main branches of one and the same tree, differ so much from one another in their formulas, now widely diffused, and yet may be so easily reconciled. These RITES are those known under the several names of the *Ancient,* that of *Heredom* or *Hairdom,* that of *the Orient of Kilwinning,* that of *St. Andrew,* that of *the Emperors of the East and West,* that of *the Princes of the Royal Secret,* or of *Perfection,* the *Philosophic* Rite, and that most recent RITE of all, known as the PRIMÆVAL.

WHEREFORE, adopting, as the basis of our conservative reformation, the title of the first of those Rites, and the number of degrees of the hierarchy of the last, WE DO DECLARE them all to be now and henceforth united and aggregated into one single ORDER, which, professing the dogma and the pure and undefiled doctrines of *the Ancient Art of Masonry,* embraces all the systems of the Scottish Rite, united together under the title of THE ANCIENT-ACCEPTED-SCOTTISH-RITE.

The entire doctrine will be communicated to Masons in thirty-three degrees divided into seven Temples, or classes, through all which every Mason must pass in regular succession, before he can arrive at the most sublime and last: and in each degree he will meet such obstructions and undergo such trials, as are required by the Institutes, Decrees and Regulations, old and new, of the ORDER and of *Perfection.*

The first degree is inferior to the second, that to the third, and so ascending regularly to the Sublime Degree (the thirty-third and last) which watches over all the others, corrects their errors and

erunt. PRINCIPES-REGII-SECRETI, in secundo et trigesimo gradu
sese collocabunt, sub SUMMIS-MAGNIS-INSPECTORIBUS-GENERALIBUS,
qui gradus tertius et trigesimus, ac ultimus ORDINIS est. Primus et trigesimus gradus *Summos-Judices-Commendatores* habebit; *Summi-Commendatores*, *Summi-Electi-Equites-Kadosch*, trigesimum gradum component. In tertio et vigesimo, ac quarto et
vigesimo, quinto et vigesimo, sexto et vigesimo, septimo et vigesimo, ac nono et vigesimo gradu, *Capita-Tabernaculi*, *Principes-
Tabernaculi*, *Equites-Serpentis-Ænei*, *Principes-Gratiœ*, *Summi-*

---

formera un SUPREME GRAND CONSEIL, dépositaire du Dogme; il
sera le *Défenseur* et le *Conservateur* de l'ORDRE qu'il gouvernera
et administrera conformément aux présentes et aux Constitutions
ci-après décrétées.

Tous les Degrés des Rites réunis, comme il est dit ci-dessus, du
premier au dix-huitième, seront classés parmi les Degrés du Rite
de *Perfection* dans leur ordre respectif et d'après l'analogie et la
similitude qui existent entr'eux; ils formeront les dix-huit premiers
Degrés du RITE ECOSSAIS ANCIEN ACCEPTÉ; le dix-neuvième Degré et le vingt-troisième Degré du Rite *Primitif* formeront le vingt-
tième Degré de l'ORDRE. Le vingtième et le vingt-troisième
Degré du Rite de *Perfection*, soit le seizième et le vingt-quatrième
Degré du Rite *Primitif* formeront le vingt-unième et le vingt-hui-
tième Degré de l'ORDRE. Les PRINCES DU ROYAL SECRET occu-
peront le trente-deuxième Degré, immédiatement au-dessous des
SOUVERAINS GRANDS INSPECTEURS GÉNÉRAUX dont le Degré sera
le trente-troisième et dernier de l'ORDRE. Le trente-unième Degré sera celui des *Souverains-Juges-Commandeurs*. Les *Grands
Commandeurs*, *Grands Elus Chevaliers Kadosch* prendront le
trentième Degré. Les *Chefs du Tabernacle*, les *Princes du Tabernacle*, les *Chevaliers du Serpent d'Airain*, les *Princes de Merci*,
les *Grands Commandeurs du Temple* et les *Grands Ecossais de
Saint-André* composeront respectivement le vingt-troisième, le
vingt-quatrième, le vingt-cinquième, le vingt-sixième, le vingt-sep-
tième et le vingt-neuvième Degré.

Tous les sublimes Degrés de ces mêmes Systèmes Ecossais réunis
seront, d'après leur analogie ou leur identité, distribués dans les
classes de leur Ordre qui correspondent au régime du RITE ÉCOS-
SAIS ANCIEN ACCEPTÉ.

Mais jamais et sous quelque prétexte que ce soit, aucun de ces

Commendatores-Templi, et *Summi-Scoti-Sancti-Andreæ* collocabuntur.

Eorumdem Scotorum Regiminum aggregatorum, omnes sublimes
gradus, secundùm eorum analogiam, vel identitatem, distributi
erunt in classes eorum Ordinis respondentes in Regimine RITUS-
SCOTICI-ANTIQUI-ACCEPTI.

Sed nunquàm, neque ullo prætextu, ullus eorum sublimium graduum adsimilari poterit Tertio et Trigesimo et Sublimissimo gradui
SUPREMI-MAGNI-INSPECTORIS-GENERALIS, PROTECTORIS, CONSERVA-

---

governs them; and a body or assembly whereof will be a GRAND
SUPREME COUNCIL absolute in matters of doctrine, *Defender* and
Conservator of THE ORDER, which it will rule and administer,
in accordance with the existing Constitutions, and those presently
to be enacted.

All the degrees of all the Rites hereby united, from the first to
the eighteenth, inclusive, will be arranged among the degrees of
the Rite of *Perfection*, each in its proper place and order, and as
analogy and similitude require, and will compose the eighteen first
degrees of THE ANCIENT ACCEPTED SCOTTISH RITE. The nine-
teenth degree and the twenty-third degree of the *Primæval* Rite,
will be the twentieth degree of the ORDER: the twentieth and
twenty-third degrees of *Perfection*, as the sixteenth and twenty-
fourth of *Primæval* Rite, will be the twenty-first and twenty-
eighth of the ORDER : THE PRINCES OF THE ROYAL SECRET
will be placed in the thirty-second degree, next below THE
SOVEREIGN GRAND INSPECTORS GENERAL, who have
the thirty-third and last degree of the ORDER. The thirty-
first degree will be that of *Sovereign Judges Commanders* and
the Sovereign Commanders, Sovereign Knights Kadosh will
constitute the thirtieth degree. The *Chiefs of the Tabernacle*,
the *Princes of the Tabernacle*, the *Knights of the Brazen
Serpent*, the *Princes of Mercy*, the *Sovereign Commanders of
the Temple*, and the *Sovereign Ecossais of Saint Andrew* will
respectively compose the twenty-third, twenty-fourth, twenty-fifth,
twenty-sixth, twenty-seventh and twenty-ninth degrees.

All the Sublime Degrees of the said several aggregated Scottish
Rites, will, according to analogy or identity, be distributed among
the classes of their ORDER, which correspond to the Regimen
of THE ANCIENT-ACCEPTED SCOTTISH RITE.

TORIS ORDINIS, ultimo ejusdem ANTIQUI-ACCEPTI-SCOTICI-RITUS ; nullo in casu poterit quis frui eisdem juribus, prærogativis, privilegiis aut facultatibus quibus eos Inspectores Nos insignimus.

Sic eos instituimus vigore facultatum supremarum et conservatricium.

Utque hoc firmum et inconcussum sit, Jubemus omnibus nostris

---

sublimes Degrés ne pourra être assimilé au trente-troisième et très Sublime Degré de SOUVERAIN GRAND INSPECTEUR GÉNÉRAL, PROTECTEUR ET CONSERVATEUR DE L'ORDRE qui est le dernier du RITE ANCIEN ACCEPTÉ ÉCOSSAIS, et, dans aucun cas, nul ne pourra jouir des mêmes droits, prérogatives, priviléges ou pouvoirs dont nous investissons ces Inspecteurs.

Ainsi nous leur conférons la plénitude de la puissance suprême et conservatrice.

Et, afin que la présente ordonnance soit fidèlement et à jamais observée, nous commandons à nos Chers, Vaillants et Sublimes Chevaliers et Princes Maçons de veiller à son exécution.

DONNÉ en notre Palais, à Berlin, le jour des Calendes—premier— de Mai, l'an de Grâce 1786, et de notre Règne le 47e.

Signé,   FRÉDÉRIC.

Dilectis, Strenuis, Excelsisque Equitibus Principibusque Latomis auxiliarem ei manum præbere.

DATUM in Nostrâ regali Sede Berolini, Calendis Maji, Anno Gratiæ MDCCLXXXVI, Nostri Regni XLVII°.

Subscriptum, "FREDERICUS."

But never, nor under any pretext whatever, can any one of those sublime degrees be assimilated to the thirty-third and most sublime degree of SOVEREIGN GRAND INSPECTOR GENERAL, PROTECTOR and CONSERVATOR of the ORDER, and the last Degree of the same ANCIENT-ACCEPTED SCOTTISH RITE: in no case can any other person enjoy those rights, prerogatives, privileges and powers wherewith We do invest those Inspectors.

And We do so institute them in the activity of such Supreme and Conservative powers.

And to the end that all hereof may remain fixed and unchanged, we do command all our well-beloved, Valiant and Noble Masonic Knights and Princes to support and maintain the same.

DONE at our Royal Residence in Berlin, this first day of May, in the year of Grace 1786, and of our Reign the 47th.

Signed, "FREDERIC."

Ad Universi Terrarum Orbis Summi Architecti Gloriam.

CONSTITUTIONES ET STATUTA

MAGNORUM SUPREMORUMQUE CONCILIORUM

CONSTANTIUM E MAGNIS GENERALIBUS INSPECTORIBUS, PATRONIS, DUCIBUS,
CONSERVATORIBUS

ORDINIS XXX^I

ULTIMIQUE GRADUS ANTIQUI·SCOTICI-RITUS-ACCEPTI

ITEM

REGULÆ

Ad Universi Terrarum Orbis Summi Architecti Gloriam.

CONSTITUTIONS ET STATUTS

DES

GRANDS ET SUPREMES CONSEILS

COMPOSÉS DES GRANDS INSPECTEURS GÉNÉRAUX, PATRONS, CHEFS ET CONSERVATEURS

DE

L'ORDRE DU 33^E

ET DERNIER DEGRÉ DU RITE ÉCOSSAIS ANCIEN ACCEPTÉ,

ET

RÈGLEMENS

POUR LE GOUVERNEMENT DE TOUS LES CONSISTOIRES, CONSEILS,
COLLÉGES, CHAPITRES ET AUTRES CORPS MACONNIQUES
SOUMIS A LA JURIDICTION DESDITS CONSEILS.

AU NOM DU TRÈS SAINT ET GRAND ARCHITECTE DE L'UNIVERS.

Ordo ab Chao.

Avec l'approbation, en la présence et sous les auspices de son Auguste Majesté Frédéric (Charles) II, Roi de Prusse, Margrave de Brandebourg, etc., très Puissant Monarque, Grand Protecteur, Grand Commandeur, etc., de l'ORDRE, etc., etc., etc.

Les Souverains Grands Inspecteurs Généraux, en Suprême Conseil assemblé,

Ont, après délibération, sanctionné les Décrets suivants qui sont et seront à perpétuité leurs CONSTITUTIONS, STATUTS ET REGLEMENS pour le gouvernement des Consistoires et autres Ateliers Maçonniques soumis à la juridiction desdits Grands Inspecteurs.

REGENDIS OMNIBUS CONSISTORIIS, CONCILIIS, COLLEGIIS, CAPITULIS,
ALIISQUE SOCIETATIBUS STRUCTORIIS EORUMDEM
CONCILIORUM JURISDICTIONI SUBJECTIS.

IN NOMINE SANCTISSIMI ET MAGNI ARCHITECTI UNIVERSI.

𝔒𝔯𝔡𝔬 𝔞𝔟 ℭ𝔥𝔞𝔬.

*Probante, præsente, sanciente Augustâ Majestate Frederici (Caroli) Secundi, Bo-
russiæ Regis, Margravii Brandeburgensis, etc., Potentissimi Monarchæ, Magni Patro-
ni, Magni Commendatoris, etc., ORDINIS, etc.,, etc., etc.*

*Magni Inspectores Supremi Universales in Supremo Concilio habito deliberaverunt,
sanciveruntque infrà exarata Decreta, quæ sunt perpetuòque erunt eorum CONSTI-
TUTIONES, STATUTA et REGULÆ regendis Consistoriis. aliisque Societatibus
structoriis eorumdem Magnorum Inspectorum jurisdictioni subjectis.*

Ad Universi Terrarum Orbis Summi Architecti Gloriam.

CONSTITUTIONS AND STATUTES

OF THE

GRAND AND SUPREME COUNCILS

COMPOSED OF GRAND INSPECTORS GENERAL, PATRONS, CHIEFS AND CONSERVATORS

OF THE

ORDER OF THE 33ᴰ

AND LAST DEGREE OF THE ANCIENT-ACCEPTED SCOTTISH RITE,

AND

REGULATIONS

FOR THE GOVERNMENT OF ALL CONSISTORIES, COUNCILS, COLLEGES,
CHAPTERS AND OTHER MASONIC BODIES UNDER THE
JURISDICTION OF SUCH COUNCILS.

IN THE NAME OF THE MOST HOLY AND GRAND ARCHITECT OF THE UNIVERSE.

𝔒𝔯𝔡𝔬 𝔞𝔟 ℭ𝔥𝔞𝔬.

*With the approval, in the presence, and with the sanction of his August Majesty
Frederic (Charles) the Second, King of Prussia, Margrave of Brandenburg, etc., Most
Potent Monarch, Grand Patron, Grand Commander, etc., of the ORDER, etc., etc., etc.*

*The Grand Supreme Universal Inspectors in Supreme Council assembled, Have de-
termined and ordained the Decrees hereunder written, which are and for ever shall be
their CONSTITUTIONS, STATUTES and REGULATIONS, for the Government
of the Consistories and other Masonic Bodies, under the jurisdiction of the said Grand
Inspectors.*

ARTICULUS I.

CONSTITUTIONUM, Statutorum, Regularumque factorum Anno MDCCLXII per novem Delegatos à Magnis Conciliis Principum Structorum à Regio Arcano, articuli omnes qui hisce non adversantur sanctionibus, servantur, et observandi erunt; qui autem adversabuntur, abrogantur, et pro expressè sublatis habentur.

ARTICULUS II.

§ I. GRADUS XXXIII, iis Structoribus qui eo legitimè ornati sunt, qualitatem, titulum, privilegium, auctoritatemque tribuit Supremorum Magnorum Generalium Ordinis Inspectorum.

ARTICLE I.

Tous les articles des CONSTITUTIONS, Statuts et Règlemens rédigés en l'année 1762 par les neuf Commissaires des Grands Conseils des Princes Maçons du Royal Secret, qui ne sont pas contraires aux présentes dispositions, sont maintenus et devront être observés ; ceux qui y sont contraires sont abrogés et considérés comme expressément abolis.

ARTICLE II.

§ I. Le trente-troisième DEGRÉ confère aux Maçons qui en sont légitimement revêtus la qualité, le titre, le privilége et l'autorité de Souverains Grands Inspecteurs Généraux de l'ORDRE.

§ II. L'objet particulier de leur mission est d'instruire et d'éclairer leurs Frères ; de faire régner parmi eux la Charité, l'Union et l'Amour fraternel ; de maintenir la régularité dans les travaux de chaque Degré et de veiller à ce qu'elle soit observée par tous les Membres ; de faire respecter, et, dans toutes les occasions, de respecter et de défendre les Dogmes, les Doctrines, les Instituts, les Constitutions, les Statuts et les Règlemens de l'ORDRE, et principalement ceux de la Haute Maçonnerie, et enfin de s'appliquer, en tous lieux, à faire des œuvres de Paix et de Miséricorde.

§ III. Une réunion de membres de ce grade prend le titre de CONSEIL DU TRENTE-TROISIEME DEGRÉ ou des PUISSANTS GRANDS INSPECTEURS GÉNÉRAUX de l'ORDRE ; ce Conseil se forme et se compose comme suit :

§ II. Eorum missionis peculiare officium est fratres docendi, et illuminandi ; Caritatem, Unionem et fraternum Amorem inter eos conservandi ; regularitatem in operibus cujuscumque gradûs servandi, utque ab aliis conservetur curandi ; Dogmata, Doctrinas, Instituta, Constitutiones, Statuta et Regulas ORDINIS, ea præcipuè Sublimis Latomiæ, ut observantiâ colantur efficiendi, eaque in occasione quâlibet servandi et defendendi ; in operibus deniquè Pacis, et Misericordiæ se ubicumquè exercendi.

§ III. Cœtus virorum ex eodem gradu, dictus *CONCILIUM TRIGESIMI TERTII* sive POTENTIUM MAGNORUM GENERALIUM INSPECTORUM ORDINIS constat, et ordinatus est proùt infrà.

ARTICLE I.

ALL the Articles of the Constitutions, Statutes, and Regulations made in the year MDCCLXII., by the nine Delegates from the Grand Councils of Princes Masons of the Royal Secret, which are not contrary to these present ordinances, are preserved in full force and shall be observed ; but such as conflict herewith are abrogated, and to be regarded as expressly repealed.

ARTICLE II.

§ I. The 33d Degree invests those Masons who are legitimately in possession thereof, with the character, title, privileges and authority of Sovereign Grand Inspectors General of the Order.

§ II. The peculiar duties entrusted to them are ;—to preserve Charity, Union and brotherly Love among them ; to maintain regularity in the work of every degree, and to take care that it is maintained by others ; to see that the Dogmas, Doctrines, Institutes, Constitutions, Statutes, and Regulations of THE ORDER, and especially those of Sublime Masonry are faithfully observed and obeyed, and on every occasion to enforce and defend them ; and every where, in fine, to do the works of Peace and Mercy.

§ III. A body of men of that degree, styled A COUNCIL OF THE 33° or of POTENT GRAND INSPECTORS *of* THE ORDER, is constituted and composed as follows :

1°. In locis aptis Supremo hujus gradûs Concilio possidendo
illi ex Inspectoribus, qui suâ admissione antiquissimus, per hæc
Decreta facultas tribuitur ad eum auctoritatis gradum alium fra-
trem elevandi, vadem se faciendo, quòd is charactere, scientiâ,
gradibusque id verè promeruerit; electique sacramentum ille
excipiet.

2°. Hi duo simùl eumdem gradum alii viro eâdem lege tribuent.

§ IV. Ità Supremum Concilium constabit.

Ex cæteris autem Candidatis, nemo admittetur, nisi omnium
suffragiorum puncta tulerit, iis suffragiis ab unoquoque viro vivâ
voce latis, incipiendo à ferentium juniore, nempè à nuperrimè omnium adscripto.

1o. Dans les lieux propres à l'établissement d'un Suprême Conseil
de ce Degré, l'Inspecteur le plus ancien en grade est, par les présentes, autorisé à élever un autre Frère à la même dignité, après
s'être assuré que celui-ci l'a réellement méritée par son caractère,
son instruction et les grades dont il est revêtu, et il lui administrera
le serment.

2o. Ces deux Frères conféreront ensemble, et de la même manière, le grade à un autre membre.

§ IV. Le Suprême Conseil sera alors constitué.

Mais aucun des autres Candidats, ne sera admis, s'il n'obtient
l'unanimité des suffrages, chaque membre donnant son vote de vive
voix, en commençant par le plus jeune, c'est-à-dire, par le dernier
reçu.

Le vote négatif d'un seul des membres délibérants, si ses raisons sont jugées suffisantes, fera rejeter le Candidat. Cette règle
sera observée dans tous les cas analogues.

ARTICLE III.

§ I. Dans les lieux ci-dessus désignés, les deux Frères qui, les
premiers, auront été élevés à ce grade, seront, *de droit*, les deux
premiers Officiers du Suprême Conseil, savoir : le très Puissant
Monarque Grand Commandeur et le très Illustre Lieutenant Grand
Commandeur.

§ II. Si le premier de ces Officiers vient à mourir, s'il abdique,
ou s'il s'absente, pour ne plus revenir, il sera remplacé par le second Officier qui choisira son successeur parmi les autres Grands
Inspecteurs.

Unius ex deliberantibus intercessio, si causa sufficiens judicabitur, Candidatum rejiciendi vim habebit. In quâlibet simili occasione hæc lex servabitur.

ARTICULUS III.

§ I. In ejusmodi regione, ut suprà, qui duo primi in eum gradum cooptati fuerint, primarii duo officiales Supremi Concilii *proprio jure* erunt: scilicet Potentissimus Monarcha Magnus Commendator, et Illustrissimus Vicarius-Magnus Commendator.

§ II. Si eorum primus obeat, abdicet dignitatem, vel è loco, nunquàm rediturus, migret, ei succedet secundus; isque in jam suum officium alium Magnum Inspectorem sibi subrogabit.

---

1. In places where a Supreme Council of this Degree may properly be established, authority is by these Decretals given to that Inspector who has been longest admitted, to elevate another Brother to the same degree and rank; he becoming the surety of such Brother, that by his character and learning, and by the degree that he possesses, he deserves such honour; and thereupon the latter shall take the oath of office.

2. Then these two, in the same manner, jointly confer the same degree on another person.

§ IV. And thus a Supreme Council will be established.

But of the subsequent Candidates, no one will be admitted, except by unanimous vote, each person voting *viva voce*, beginning with the junior member,—that is, the one last received.

The negative vote of one of the Inspectors, if the cause assigned therefor shall be adjudged sufficient, shall reject the Candidate. And this shall be the rule in all similar cases.

ARTICLE III.

§ I. The two Brethren who first receive that degree, in such a place as aforesaid, shall be *of right* the two first officers of The Supreme Council; to wit, the Most Potent Monarch Grand Commander, and the Most Illustrious Deputy Grand Commander.

§ II. If the former of these officers die, resign, or remove from the place, without the intention of returning, the latter shall succeed to his office, and shall thereupon appoint another Grand Inspector to fill his own place thus vacated.

§ III. Si secundus Magistus officium dimittit, diem obit, vel perpetuò absens fit, successionem in ejus officium primus Magistratus alteri ejusdem gradûs fratri destinabit.

§ IV. Potentissimus Monarcha pariter eliget Illustrem Ministrum Statûs Sancti Imperii, Illustrem Cæremoniarum Magnum Magistrum, Illustrem Custodiarum Ducem ; destinabitque eodem modo viros cæteris muneribus quæ vacua erunt, vel esse poterunt.

ARTICULUS IV.

QUISQUE Structor qui, dotibus et idoneitate quæ requiruntur, ornatus, in eum Sublimem Gradum adscribetur, solvet anteà in manibus Illustrissimi Thesaurarii Sancti Imperii, dotationem *decem Frederi-*

---

§ III. Si le second Ôfficier abdique, s'il meurt ou s'il s'éloigne pour toujours, le premier Officier lui donnera pour successeur un autre Frère du même grade.

§ IV. Le très Puissant Monarque nommera également l'Illustre Ministre d'État du Saint Empire, l'Illustre Grand-Maître des Cérémonies et l'Illustre Capitaine des Gardes et il désignera, de la même manière, des Frères pour remplir les autres emplois vacants ou qui pourront le devenir.

ARTICLE IV.

TOUT Maçon qui, possédant les qualités et les capacités requises, sera élevé à ce Grade Sublime, paiera préalablement, entre les mains du très Illustre Trésorier du Saint Empire, une contribution de *dix Frédérics d'or* ou de *dix Louis d'or*, *monnaie ancienne*, ou l'équivalent en argent du pays.

Lorsqu'un Frère sera initié au trentième, au trente-unième ou au trente-deuxième Degré, on exigera de lui une somme de pareille valeur et même titre, pour chaque grade.

Le SUPRÊME CONSEIL surveillera l'administration de ces fonds et en disposera dans l'intérêt de l'ORDRE.

ARTICLE V.

§ I. TOUT SUPRÊME CONSEIL se composera de neuf Souverains Grands Inspecteurs Généraux du trente-troisième Degré, dont quatre, au moins, devront professer la religion dominante du pays.

corum aureorum, sive *veterum aureorum Ludovicorum*, aut quod in monetâ loci tantumdem valeat.

Quando trigesimo gradui, vel trigesimo primo, vel trigesimo secundo aliquis fratrum initiabitur, ab eo pro quolibet gradu eadem pecuniæ summa, iisdem modo et titulo, exigetur.

SUPREMUM CONCILIUM ad hanc administrationem advigilabit, summarumque usum pro ORDINIS utilitate diriget.

ARTICULUS V.

§ I. *Supremum Concilium* quodlibet constabit ex novem Magnis-Inspectoribus-Generalibus XXXIII¹ gradûs, quorum saltem quatuor maximè extentam religionem profiteri debebunt.

---

§ III. If such second officer resign, die, or permanently remove, the first officer shall fill the vacancy so occurring, by appointment of another Brother of the same degree.

§ IV. The Most Potent Monarch will also appoint the Illustrious Minister of State of the Holy Empire, the Illustrious Grand Master of Ceremonies, and the Illustrious Captain of the Guards; and fill such other offices, by appointment, as are or may become vacant.

ARTICLE IV.

EVERY Mason, who, being found to possess the endowments and skill that are required, shall be advanced to that sublime degree, shall first pay into the hands of the Most Illustrious Treasurer of the Holy Empire, a donation of *ten Frederics d'or*, or *ten Louis d'or of the old issue*, or what, in the local currency, shall be equivalent thereto.

Whenever any Brother is initiated into the thirtieth, thirty-first or thirty-second degree, he shall be required to pay, for each such degree, the same sum of money in the same coin, or its equivalent.

THE SUPREME COUNCIL will administer the fund thus created, and direct its use in such manner as shall be most to the advantage of THE ORDER.

ARTICLE V.

§ I. EVERY SUPREME COUNCIL shall consist of nine Grand Inspectors General of the 33d Degree; four of whom, at least, must profess the religion that most generally prevails—in the particular country where it is established.

§ II. Ubi Potentissimus Monarcha Magnus Commendator, et Locum-tenens Magnus Commendator ORDINIS adsint, tribus Membris Concilium efficitur, satisque est ad ORDINIS negotia gerenda.

§ III. In Europæ magnâ quâque Natione, unoquoque Regno aut Imperio, unicum Supremum Concilium ejusdem gradûs erit.

In Statibus et Provinciis, ex quibus, tàm in Continenti terrâ quàm in Insulis, Septentrionalis America constat, duo erunt Concilia, unum ab altero tàm longè sita, quàm fieri poterit.

Item in Statibus Provinciisque, seu in Continenti terrâ, seu in Insulis, Meridionalem Americam componentibus, duo quoque Concilia erunt, unum ab altero quàm fieri poterit, remotissima.

---

§ II. Lorsque le très Puissant Monarque Grand Commandeur et le Lieutenant Grand Commandeur de l'ORDRE sont présents, trois membres suffisent pour composer le Suprême Conseil et pour l'expédition des affaires de l'ORDRE.

§ III. Dans chaque grande Nation, Royaume ou Empire d'Europe, il n'y aura qu'un seul Suprême Conseil de ce grade.

Dans les États et Provinces dont se compose l'Amérique Septentrionale, soit sur le continent, soit dans les îles, il y aura deux Conseils, aussi éloignés que possible l'un de l'autre.

Dans les États et Provinces dont se compose l'Amérique Méridionale, soit sur le continent, soit dans les îles, il y aura également ment deux Conseils, aussi éloignés que possible l'un de l'autre.

Il n'y aura qu'un seul Suprême Conseil dans chaque Empire, Etat Souverain ou Royaume d'Asie, d'Afrique, etc., etc.

ARTICLE VI.

LE Suprême Conseil n'exerce pas toujours directement son autorité sur les Degrés au-dessous du dix-septième ou *Chevalier d'Orient et d'Occident*. D'après les circonstances et les localités, il peut la déléguer même tacitement ; mais son droit est imprescriptible, et toutes les Loges et tous les Conseils de Parfaits Maçons, de quelque degré que ce soit, sont, par les présentes, requis de reconnaître, dans ceux qui sont revêtus du trente-troisième Degré, l'autorité des Souverains Grands Inspecteurs Généraux de l'ORDRE, de respecter leurs prérogatives, de leur rendre les honneurs qui leur sont dus, de leur obéir, et enfin, de déférer avec confiance à toutes les demandes qu'ils pourraient formuler pour le bien de l'ORDRE, en vertu de ses lois, des présentes Grandes Constitutions et

Unum tantum erit in quolibet Imperio, Statu Supremo, aut Regno, in Asià, in Africâ, etc., etc.

ARTICULUS VI.

SUPREMUM CONCILIUM non semper auctoritatem suam directè exercet in gradus subter XVII^m, seu *Orientis et Occidentis Equitem*. Proùt conveniet, et secundùm loca potest eam demandare, idque etiam tacitè; sed suum jus impræscriptibile est; et à quâlibet Latomiâ et à Concilio quolibet Perfectorum Structorum cujus-cumque gradûs fuerit, præsentes requirunt, ut in trigesimi tertii gradûs viris, munus Magnorum Generalium ORDINIS Inspectorum

---

§ II. When the Most Potent Sovereign Grand Commander and the Deputy Grand Commander of THE ORDER are present, three members will constitute a Council, competent to transact the business of THE ORDER.

§ III. In each of the Great Nations of Europe, whether Kingdom or Empire, there shall be but a single Supreme Council of the 33d Degree.

In all those States and Provinces, as well of the main-land as of the Islands, whereof North America is composed, there shall be two Councils, one at as great a distance as may be from the other.

In all those States and Provinces also, whether of the Main-land or the Islands, whereof South America is composed, there shall be two Councils, oue at as great a distance as possible from the other.

Likewise there shall be one only in each Empire, Supreme State or Kingdom, in Asia, in Africa, &c., &c.

ARTICLE VI.

A SUPREME COUNCIL need not always exercise its authority directly, over the degrees below the 17th, or *Knight of the East and West*. When convenience and locality make it proper, it may delegate that power of government, and that even tacitly and by implication; but there can be no prescription against its right: and these presents do require of every Lodge and Council of Perfect Masons, of whatever degree, that in those who have at-tained the 33d degree, they recognize their rank and office of Grand Inspectors General of THE ORDER, that they do respect their prerogatives, pay them due honour, be obedient to them, and read-ily comply with whatever they may require, for the good of THE

agnoscant, illorum prærogativas observent, debitum honorem illis
tribuant, iis obediant, deniquè ut cum fiduciâ postulatis omnibus
obsequantur, quæ ab illis fieri poterint, pro ORDINIS commodi-
tate, in vim ejus legum, præsentium Magnarum Constitutionum,
munerumque iis Inspectoribus propriorum, sive generalium, sive
specialium, temporalium etiam et personalium.

ARTICULUS VII.

OMNIA CONCILIA, Structoresque omnes in gradu suprà XVI^m
constituti, jus habent SUPREMUM CONCILIUM Supremorum Inspectorum appellandi ; quod permittere poterit appellantes præstò
adesse, præsentesque audiri.

---

de l'autorité dévolue à ces Inspecteurs, que cette autorité soit générale ou spéciale, ou même temporaire et personnelle.

ARTICLE VII.

TOUT CONSEIL et tout Maçon d'un grade au-dessus du seizième,
ont le droit d'en appeler au SUPRÊME CONSEIL des Souverains Grands
Inspecteurs Généraux, qui pourra leur permettre de se présenter
devant lui et de se faire entendre en personne.

Quand il s'agira d'une *affaire d'honneur* entre des Maçons, de
quelque grade qu'ils soient, la cause sera portée directement devant
le SUPRÊME CONSEIL qui décidera en première et dernière instance.

ARTICLE VIII.

UN GRAND CONSISTOIRE de Princes Maçons du Royal Secret
choisira son Président parmi les membres du trente-deuxième degré qui le composent ; mais, dans tous les cas, les actes d'un Grand
Consistoire n'auront de valeur qu'autant qu'ils auront été préalablement sanctionnés par le SUPRÊME CONSEIL du trente-troisième Degré, qui, après la mort de son Auguste Majesté le Roi, très Puissant
Monarque et Commandeur Général de l'ORDRE, héritera de l'autorité Suprême Maçonnique et l'exercera dans toute l'étendue de
l'Etat, du Royaume ou de l'Empire qui aura été placé sous sa
juridiction.

Ubi de *honore contentio* sit inter Structores, cujuscumque gradûs sint, causa directè feretur ad SUPREMUM CONCILIUM quod in primâ eâdemque ultimâ instantiâ judicabit.

ARTICULUS VIII.

MAGNUM CONSISTORIUM Principum Structorum à Regio Arcano, trigesimi secundi gradûs, virum ex proprio ordine in præsidem sibi eliget ; sed, quocumque in casu, ex ejus nullum Consistorii actis vim habebit nisi præviâ sanctione SUPREMI CONCILII XXXIII[1] gradûs, quod, Augustæ Majestatis Rege, Potentissimo Monarchâ, Commendatore Universali ORDINIS vitâ functo, in Supremâ Structoriâ auctoritate hæres erit, ad eam exercendam in amplitudine Statûs, Regni, aut Imperii pro quo fuerit instituta.

ORDER, to enforce its laws, these present Grand Constitutions, and the powers that to those Inspectors appertain, whether general or special, and even temporary and personal.

ARTICLE VII.

ALL COUNCILS, and all bodies of Masons possessed of any degree above the 16th, have the right to appeal to THE SUPREME COUNCIL of Sovereign Inspectors General; which may allow the appellants to come before it, and being present to be heard.

In case of any *affair of honor* among Masons of whatever degree, the matter shall be directly brought before THE SUPREME COUNCIL, whose jurisdiction in such case shall be original, and its decision final.

ARTICLE VIII.

GRAND CONSISTORIES of Princes-Masons of the Royal Secret, of the 32d degree, shall each elect for their President one of their own members; but in no case can any of the Decretals of any such Consistory be in force, without the previous sanction of THE SUPREME COUNCIL of the 33d Degree ; each of which Councils, upon the decease of His August Majesty the King, now the Most Potent Sovereign and Universal Commander of THE ORDER, will succeed to the Supreme Masonic authority, and exercise the same throughout the whole extent of the State, Kingdom, or Empire wherefor it is constituted.

ARTICULUS IX.

IN regione subjectâ jurisdictioni SUPREMI CONCILII Supremorum Generalium, Inspectorum, debitè constituti, *ab aliisque omnibus recogniti*, nullus Supremus Magnus Inspector Generalis, aut Delegatus-Inspector-Generalis, suâ auctoritate uti poterit, nisi ipse ab eodem SUPREMO CONCILIO recognitus approbatusque fuerit.

ARTICULUS X.

NULLUS Deputatus-Inspector-Generalis, seu jàm admissus et Diplomate insignitus, seu qui juxtá hanc Constitutionem in posterum admittetur, poterit singulari suâ auctoritate conferre gradum *Equitis Kadosch*, seu superiorem illi, vel de eâ re Diplomata alicui, quicumque sit, concedere.

ARTICLE IX. *

DANS les pays soumis à la juridiction d'un SUPRÊME CONSEIL de Souverains Grands Inspecteurs Généraux, régulièrement constitué, ET RECONNU PAR TOUS LES AUTRES SUPRÊMES CONSEILS, AUCUN Souverain Grand Inspecteur Général ou Député Inspecteur Général *ne pourra faire usage de son autorité*, à moins qu'il n'ait été reconnu par ce même SUPRÊME CONSEIL et qu'il n'ait obtenu son approbation.

ARTICLE X.

AUCUN Député-Inspecteur-Géneral, soit qu'il ait été déjà admis et pourvu d'une patente, soit qu'en vertu des présentes Constitutions il soit ultérieurement admis, ne pourra, de son autorité privée, conférer à qui que ce soit le Degré de *Chevalier Kadosch* ou tout autre degré supérieur, ni en donner des patentes.

ARTICLE XI.

LE Degré de *Chevalier Kadosch*, ainsi que le trente-unième et le trente-deuxième Degré, ne sera conféré qu'à des Maçons qui en auront été jugés dignes, et ce, en présence de trois Souverains Grands Inspecteurs Généraux au moins.

ARTICLE XII.

LORSQU'IL plaira au très Saint et Grand Architecte de l'Univers d'appeler à LUI son Auguste Majesté le Roi, très Puissant Souverain Grand Protecteur, Commandeur et Véritable Conservateur de l'ORDRE, etc., etc., etc., chaque SUPREME CONSEIL de Souverains Grands Inspecteurs Généraux, déjà régulièrement constitué et

ARTICULUS XI.

GRADUS *Equitis Kadosch*, item XXXI* et XXXII*, non tribuentur nisi Structoribus, qui iis digni fuerint judicati, præsentibusque saltem tribus Supremis Magnis Inspectoribus Generalibus.

ARTICULUS XII.

IN eo puncto temporis quo Sanctissimo Magnoque Universi Architecto placebit ad se vocare Augustæ Majestatis Regem, Potentissimum Supremum Magnum ORDINIS Patronum, Commendatorem, Verumque Conservatorem, etc., etc., etc., unumquodque SUPREMUM CONCILIUM Supremorum Majorum Generalium Inspectorum, seu nunc debitè constitutum et recognitum, seu quod

---

ARTICLE IX.

IN a country under the jurisdiction of a SUPREME COUNCIL of Sovereign Inspectors General, which has been duly constituted, and is *recognized by all the other Councils,* no Sovereign Grand Inspector General, or Deputy Inspector General can exercise his individual powers, unless he shall have been recognized and confirmed by such SUPREME COUNCIL.

ARTICLE X.

No Deputy Inspector General, whether heretofore admitted as such and furnished with his Diploma, or whether hereafter admitted, agreeably to this Constitution, can of his own individual authority confer the degree of *Knight Kadosh,* or any degree higher than that, or grant to any person whatever the Diploma of either such degree.

ARTICLE XI.

THE degree of *Knight Kadosh,* and the 31st and 32d degrees, can only be conferred on such Masons as shall have been adjudged worthy thereof, and at a meeting of, and by, at least three Sovereign Grand Inspectors General.

ARTICLE XII.

AT whatever moment it shall please the Most Holy and Grand Architect of the Universe to take to Himself His August Majesty the King, the Most Potent Sovereign Grand Patron, Commander and True Defender of THE ORDER, &c., &c., &c., each SUPREME COUNCIL of Sovereign Grand Inspectors General, whether now duly

in vim horum Statutorum institutum recognitumque in posterum
fuerit, fiet pleno jure legitimè præditum totâ illâ Structoriâ Auctoritate quam nunc Augusta Majestas Sua possidet ; eâque auctoritate
Concilium quodque utetur cùm opus fuerit et ubicumquè, in totâ
amplitudine regionis suæ Jurisdictioni subjectæ ; eùmque vel quoàd
Diplomata, vel quoàd Auctoritatem Inspectorum Generalium Depu-
tatorum, vel quoàd aliud, causa ad protestandum de illegalitate
emerget, relatio de hoc fiet, quæ Supremis Conciliis Universis
amborum Hemisphæriorum mittetur.

ARTICULUS XIII.

§ I. Supremum Concilium XXXIII[1] gradûs poterit unum

reconnu, ou qui serait ultérieurement constitué et reconnu en vertu
des présents Statuts, sera, de plein droit, légitimement investi de
toute l'autorité Maçonnique dont son Auguste Majesté est actuel-
lement revêtue. Chaque Suprême Conseil exercera cette autorité
lorsqu'il sera nécessaire et en quelque lieu que ce soit, dans toute
l'étendue du pays soumis à sa juridiction ; et si, pour cause d'illé-
galité, il y a lieu de protester, soit qu'il s'agisse des Patentes ou
des pouvoirs accordés aux Députés Inspecteurs Généraux, ou de
tout autre sujet, on en fera un rapport qui sera adressé à tous les
Suprêmes Conseils des deux hémisphères.

ARTICLE XIII.

§ I. Tout Suprême Conseil du trente-troisième Degré pourra
déléguer un ou plusieurs des Souverains Grands Inspecteurs Généraux de l'ORDRE qui le composent, pour fonder, constituer
et établir un Conseil du même degré dans tous les pays mention-
nés dans les présents Statuts, à la condition qu'ils obéiront ponc-
tuellement à ce qui est stipulé dans le troisième paragraphe de l'article II ci-dessus, ainsi qu'aux autres dispositions de la présente
Constitution.

§ II. Le Suprême Conseil pourra également donner à ces Députés le pouvoir d'accorder des patentes aux Députés Inspecteurs
Généraux, qui devront au moins avoir reçu régulièrement tous les
degrés que possède un Chevalier Kadosch, leur déléguant telle portion de leur autorité suprême qu'il sera nécessaire pour constituer,
diriger et surveiller les Loges et les Conseils, du quatrième au
vingt-neuvième Dégré inclusivement, *dans les pays où il n'y aura*

pluresve è suis membris Supremis Magnis Inspectoribus Generalibus ORDINIS, Legatos mittere fundatum, constitutum, firmatum Concilium ejusdem Gradûs in aliquâ regionum in hisce Statutis descriptarum ; eâ lege ut ii accuratè pareant eo quod in tertio paragrapho præcedentis Articuli secundi decretum est, aliisque Constitutionis hujus sanctionibus.

§ II. Poterit quoque eisdem Legatis facultatem tribuere emittendi Diplomata delegantia Deputatis Inspectoribus-Generalibus — saltem gradibus omnibus Equitis Kadosch regulariter insignitis, — partem plenarum facultatum, ut possint statuere, dirigere, et observare Latomias, et Concilia gradu à IV ° ad XXIX ᵐ inclusivè, *in*

---

constituted and recognized, or which may hereafter, by virtue of these Statutes, be constituted and recognized, will, of full right, become possessed of the entirety of that Masonic authority wherewith His August Majesty is now invested; and each may thenceforward exercise that authority, whenever necessary, and everywhere soever, throughout the whole extent of country under its jurisdiction : and whenever there may be occasion for protest, or grounds of illegality, in regard to Diplomas, or to the authority of Deputy Inspectors General, or to any other matter or thing, let a statement thereof be drawn up, and transmitted to all the SUPREME COUNCILS of both Hemispheres.

ARTICLE XIII.

§ I. EACH SUPREME COUNCIL of the 33d Degree may delegate one or more of the Sovereign Grand Inspectors General of THE ORDER, its members, to found, constitute and establish a Council of the same degree, in any of the Countries mentioned in the Statutes; those Deputies punctually obeying the law contained in the third paragraph of the preceding article second, and the other provisions of this Constitution.

§ II. Each such Supreme Council may also authorize such Deputies to grant Diplomas, delegating to Deputy Inspectors General, —who must regularly have received all the degrees, at least, of which a Knight Kadosh should be possessed—so much of their plenary powers, as may enable them to establish, regulate and superintend Lodges and Councils in any of the Degrees, from the 4th

locis ubi non erunt Sublimis Gradús Latomiæ vel Concilia legitinè instituta.

§ III. Rituale manuscriptum Sublimium Graduum nemini alii tradetur quàm duobus primis cujusque Concilii Officialibus, vel fratri qui in aliquam regionem mittetur ut eorumdem Concilium ibi instituat.

ARTICULUS XIV.

In quâlibet Sublimium Graduum cæremoniâ structoriâ, et solemni virorum in iis gradibus constitutorum processù, Supremum Con-cilium cæteros sequetur, omniumque membrorum ultimi erunt pri-marii duo Magistratus; hosque Magnum Vexillum, et Gladius ORDINIS immediatè præcedent.

---

point d'ateliers ou de Conseils du Sublime *Degré* légalement cons-titués.

§ III. Le Rituel manuscrit des Sublimes Degrés ne sera confié qu'aux deux premiers Officiers de chaque Conseil ou qu'à un Frère chargé de constituer un Conseil des mêmes Degrés dans un autre pays.

ARTICLE XIV.

Dans toute cérémonie maçonnique des Sublimes Degrés et dans toute procession solennelle de Maçons possédant ces degrés, le Suprême Conseil marchera le dernier et les deux premiers Offi-ciers se placeront après tous les autres membres et seront immédia-tement précédés du grand Étendard et du Glaive de l'ORDRE.

ARTICLE XV.

§ I. Un Suprême Conseil doit se réunir régulièrement dans les trois premiers jours de chaque troisième nouvelle lune ; il s'assem-blera plus souvent, si les affaires de l'ORDRE l'exigent et si l'expé-dition en est urgente.

§ II. Outre les grandes fêtes solennelles de l'ORDRE, le Su-prême Conseil en aura trois particulières chaque année, savoir : le jour des Calendes—premier d'Octobre, le vingt-sept de Décem-bre et le jour des Calendes—premier de Mai.

ARTICLE XVI.

§ I. Pour être reconnu et pour jouir des priviléges attachés au treute-troisième Degré, chaque Souverain Grand Inspecteurs Gé-néral sera muni de Patentes et de lettres de Créance dont le mo-

ARTICULUS XV.

§ I. Supremum Concilium regulariter haberi debet per triduum quo tertium quodque novilunium incipit; frequentiùs convocabitur, si id negotia ORDINIS postulent eorumque transactio urgeat.

§ II. Ultrà magnos solemnesque festos ORDINIS dies, Supremium Concilium quoque anno sibi peculiares tres sacros habebit; nempè Calendas Octobris, vigesimum septimum Decembris, Calendasque Majas.

ARTICULUS XVI.

§ I. Supremus quisque Inspector-Magnus-Generalis ut agnoscatur, privilegiisque XXXIII° gradui annexis frui possit, præditus erit Patentibus et Credentialibus Litteris emissis ad normam præs-

---

to the 29th inclusive, *in places where there are no Lodges or Councils of the Sublime Degree,* legally constituted.

§ III. The manuscript Ritual of the Sublime Degrees shall be entrusted only to the two highest Officers of each Council, or to a Brother commissioned to establish elsewhere a Council of those Degrees.

ARTICLE XIV.

In every Masonic Ceremony of the Sublime Degrees, and every solemn procession of those invested with such degrees, THE SUPREME COUNCIL is in the rear, and the two highest Officers in the rear of all the Members; with the great Banner and the Sword of THE ORDER immediately preceding them.

ARTICLE XV.

§ I. A Supreme Council should regularly be held during the three days wherewith each third new-moon commences: and will be more frequently convened, if the business of THE ORDER, to be transacted, require it.

§ II. In addition to the great and solemn feast-days of THE ORDER, each Supreme Council will have three sacred days in every year, peculiar to itself,—the 1st of October, the 27th of December, and the 1st of May.

ARTICLE XVI.

§ I. That each Sovereign Grand Inspector General may be recognized, and be enabled to enjoy the privileges attached to the 33d Degree, he shall be furnished with Patents and Letters of

cripti in ejusdem gradûs Rituali ; quæ Litteræ ipsi tradentur eâ conditione ut solvat Thesauro Sancti Imperii pretium quod SUPREMUM CONCILIUM unumquodque pro suâ jurisdictione, ubi primùm institutum fuerit, taxabit.   Solvet item is Magnus-Supremus-Inspector-Generalis Illustri Viro ab epistolis, in præmium laboris pro expeditione Litterarum et appositionis Sigilli, unum Fredericum, sive vet erem Ludovicum, vel id pecuniæ, quod in monetâ loci tatumdem valeat.

§ II. Quilibet Magnus Inspector Generalis habebit insuper suorum actorum codicem, cujus quæque pagina numero distincta sit ; prima insuper atque ultima speciali adnotatione tales esse designabuntur.   In eo codice inscribi debebunt Magnæ Constitutiones, Statuta et Generales Regulæ Sublimis Structoriæ Artis.

---

dèle se trouve dans le Rituel du Degré. Ces Lettres lui seront délivrées à la condition de verser dans le Trésor du Saint Empire la somme que chaque SUPRÊME CONSEIL fixera pour sa juridiction aussitôt qu'il aura été constitué. Ledit Souverain Grand Inspecteur Général paiera également un Frédéric, ou un Louis, monnaie ancienne, ou l'équivalent en argent du pays, à l'Illustre Secrétaire, en compensation de sa peine, pour l'expédition desdites Lettres et pour l'apposition du Sceau.

§ II. Tout Souverain Grand Inspecteur Général tiendra, en outre, un Registre de ses Actes : chaque page en sera numérotée ; la première et la dernière pages seront quotées et paraphées pour en constater l'identité. On devra transcrire sur ce Registre les Grandes Constitutions, les Statuts et les Règlemens Généraux de l'Art Sublime de la Franche-Maçonnerie.

L'Inspecteur lui-même sera tenu d'y inscrire successivement tous ses Actes, à peine de nullité ou même d'interdiction.

Les Députés Inspecteurs Généraux sont tenus d'agir de même sous les mêmes peines.

§ III. Ils se montreront mutuellement leurs Registres et leurs Patentes, et ils y constateront réciproquement les lieux où ils se seront rencontrés et reconnus.

ARTICLE XVII.

LA MAJORITÉ des voix est nécessaire pour légaliser les actes des Souverains Grands Inspecteurs Généraux, dans les lieux où il existe un SUPRÊME CONSEIL du trente-troisième Degré, légalement constitué et reconnu. En conséquence, dans un pays, ou territoire sous la dé-

Inspector ipse tenebitur ad ordinatè describendum in eo omnia sua acta, sub pœnâ nullitatis atque etiam interdictionis.

Deputati Inspectores Generales ad id, sub pœnis iisdem, tenentur.

§ III. Ipsi sibi mutuò ostendent Codices et Diplomata, in iisque mutuò adnotabunt loca ubi unus alteri occurrerit et se invicem recognoverint.

ARTICULUS XVII.

MAJORI suffragiorum numero est opus ad tribuendam legalem auctoritatem actis Supremorum Majorum Generalium Inspectorum, in eo loco ubi extat SUPREMUM CONCILIUM XXXIII[1] gradûs, *legitimè institutum et recognitum.* Quapropter, in eâ regione, vel eo

---

Credence, issued in the form prescribed in the Ritual of that Degree: which Letters will be given him, on his paying into the Treasury of the Holy Empire, such sum as each SUPREME COUNCIL may fix for its jurisdiction, immediately after its establishment. Such Sovereign Grand Inspector General will also pay to the Illustrious Secretary, as his fee for expediting the Letters and affixing the Seal, a Frédéric d'or or a Louis d'or of the old issue, or so much in the currency of the place as may be equivalent thereto.

§ II. Every Grand Inspector General will moreover keep a Register of all his acts, each page whereof will be separately and regularly numbered, and the first and last pages be specially designated as such. In this Register must be copied the Grand Constitutions, Statutes, and General Regulations of the Sublime Art of Masonry.

Each Inspector must enter in his Register everything done by him, in its regular order, on pain of nullity and even of interdict.

Deputy Inspectors General are bound to do the same, under the same penalty.

§ III. They will mutually exhibit to each other their Registers and Patents, and note in their Respective Registers the place where one meets the other, and where they recognize each other.

ARTICLE XVII.

IT requires a majority of votes to invest with legal authority the acts of individual Sovereign Grand Inspectors General, done in a jurisdiction where there exists a SUPREME COUNCIL of the 33d Degree, *duly constituted and recognized.* Wherefore, in whatever

territorio quod ab ejusmodi Concilio dependeat, NEMO eorum Inspectorum suâ auctoritate singulariter uti poterit, nisi in casu quo
ab eodem Supremo Concilio facultatem impetraverit, vel, si Inspector ad aliam jurisdictionem pertineat, non obtinuerit admission-
em eo rescripto, quod à formulâ Exequatur nomen habet.

ARTICULUS XVIII.

Summæ omnes ad expensas subeundas receptæ—*tributa nempè
pro admissione*—quæ titulo initiationis gradibus suprà XVI ^{m} ad
XXXIII ^{m} inclusum, exiguntur, mittentur in thesaurum Sancti Imperii, curantibus Præsidibus et Thesaurariis Conciliorum, Sublimi-
umque Latomiarum eorumdem graduum, Supremis Magnis Inspec-

---

pendance d'un Suprême Conseil, aucun de ces Inspecteurs ne
pourra exercer individuellement son autorité, à moins d'en avoir
obtenu l'autorisation dudit Suprême Conseil, et, dans le cas où
l'Inspecteur appartiendrait à une autre Juridiction, à moins d'avoir
été reconnu par une déclaration à laquelle la formule a fait donner
le nom d'Exéquatur.

ARTICLE XVIII.

Toutes les sommes reçues pour faire face aux dépenses,—*c'est-à-
dire le prix des Réceptions*,—et qui se perçoivent à titre de frais
d'initiation aux Degrés au-dessus du seizième jusques et y compris
le trente-troisième, seront versées dans le Trésor du Saint Empire,
à la diligence des Présidents et Trésoriers des Conseils et des
Loges Sublimes de ces Degrés, ainsi que des Souverains Grands
Inspecteurs Généraux, de leurs Députés, de l'Illustre Secrétaire et
de l'Illustre Trésorier du Saint Empire.

Le Suprême Conseil réglera et surveillera l'administration et
l'emploi de ces sommes : il s'en fera rendre, chaque année, un
compte exact et fidèle, et il aura soin d'en faire part aux ateliers
de sa dépendance.

ARRETÉ, FAIT et APPROUVÉ en Grand et Suprême
Conseil du trente-troisième Degré, régulièrement constitué, convoqué et assemblé, avec l'approbation et en présence de sa très
Auguste Majesté, FRÉDÉRIC, deuxième du nom, par la grâce
de Dieu, Roi de Prusse, Margrave de Brandebourg, etc., etc., etc.,

toribus Generalibus, eorumque Deputatis, nec non Illustri Viro à Secretis, Illustrique Thesaurario Sancti Imperii.

Earum summarum administratio et usus dirigentur et observabuntur à SUPREMO CONCILIO; quod efficiet ut quoque anno rationes fideliter absolutèque ei reddantur; hasque communicari curabit Societatibus omnibus ab eo dependentibus.

DELIBERATUM, ACTUM, SANCITUM in MAGNO ET SUPREMO CONCILIO XXXIII' gradûs debitè instituto, indicto, atque habito cum probatione et præsentiâ Augustissimæ MAJESTATIS, FREDERICI, nomine secundi, Deo favente, Regis Borussiæ, Margravii Brandeburgi, etc., etc., etc., Potentissimi Monarchæ, Magni Pa-

---

region or territory is of the dependencies of such a Council, no such Inspector can individually exercise any power, unless he has first obtained authority from such SUPREME COUNCIL; or, if he belong to another jurisdiction, until he has been empowered by that authorization, which from its phraseology is termed an EXEQUATUR.

ARTICLE XXVIII.

ALL moneys received as revenue—*to wit, the fees for conferring the degrees*—and which are demandable for such degrees from the 16th to the 33d inclusive, shall be deposited in the Treasury of the Holy Empire, in the custody and care of the Presiding Officers and Treasurers of the Councils and Sublime Lodges of those Degrees, and of the Sovereign Grand Inspectors General and their Deputies, the Illustrious Secretary and the Illustrious Treasurer of the Holy Empire.

The disbursement and expenditure of such moneys are to be directed and controlled by THE SUPREME COUNCIL; which will see to it that full and correct accounts thereof are rendered in each year; and those accounts it will cause to be communicated to all its subordinate Bodies.

SETTLED, DONE, AND RATIFIED, in GRAND AND SUPREME COUNCIL of the 33d Degree, duly constituted, convoked and held; present and approving His August MAJESTY FREDERIC the Second, by the grace of God, King of Prussia, Margrave of Brandenburg, &c., &c., &c., most potent Sovereign, Grand

troni, Magni Commendatoris, Magni Magistri Universalis Verique Conservatoris ORDINIS.

Calendis Maji A. L. ICCDCCLXXXVI et à Christo nato MDCCLXXXVI.

(Subscriptum) "......(*)......" — "STARK." —".......(*)

---

très Puissant Monarque, Grand Protecteur, Grand Commandeur, Grand Maître Universel et Véritable Conservateur de l'ORDRE.

Le jour des Calendes—premier de Mai, A. L. 5786, et de l'ère Chrétienne 1786.

Signé ".....(*).....» — "STARK." — ".......(*) ....."
— "...... (*) ......" — " H. WILLHELM. " — " D'ESTERNO. "
— "...... (*) ......" — " WŒLLNER. "

APPROUVÉ et donné en notre Résidence Royale de Berlin, le jour des Calendes—premier de Mai, l'an de Grâce 1786, et de notre règne le 47°.

    L. S.   *Signé,*   FRÉDÉRIC.

......" — ".......(*)......" — " H. WILLELM." — " D'ES-
TERNO." — "......(*)......" — " WŒLLNER."

APPROBATUM datumque in nostrâ Regali Residentiâ Berolini,
Calendis Maji, Anno Gratiæ MDCCLXXXVI, Nostrique Regni
XLVII.

   L. S.   Subscriptum,   FREDERICUS.

(*) *Vide notam in fine.*

Patron, Grand Commander, Universal Grand Master, and True
Defender, of THE ORDER.

The first day of May, A.·. L.·. 5786, and C.·. E.·. 1786.

(*Signed*) "......(*)......" — " STARK." — "......(*)......"
—"......(*)......"—" H. WILLELM."—" D'ESTERNO."—"......
(*)......" — " WŒLLNER."

APPROVED and done at our Royal Residence in Berlin, the first
day of May, in the year of Grace 1786, and of our Reign the 47th.

   (L.·. S.·.)   *Signed,*   FREDERIC.

(*) *See the note at the conclusion.*

Appendix.

APPENDIX

STATUTA FUNDAMENTALIA MAGNASQUE CONSTITUTIONES
SUPREMI CONCILII TRIGESIMI TERTII GRADUS.

ARTICULUS I.

VEXILLUM ORDINIS est argenteum* circumdatum aureâ fimbriâ, habens in medio bicipitem Aquilam nigram, alas tenentem extensas, habentem aureum rostrum, aurea crura, distringentemque altero pede aureum capulum, altero ferrum antiqui gladii juxtà horizontis directionem jacentis et è dextrâ in sinistram versi ; ab hoc gladio

* *Album.*

APPENDICE

STATUTS FONDAMENTAUX ET GRANDES CONSTITUTIONS
DU SUPREME CONSEIL DU TRENTE-TROISIEME DEGRÉ.

ARTICLE I.

L'ÉTENDARD de l'ORDRE est *argent** frangé d'or, portant au centre un aigle noir à deux têtes, les ailes déployées ; les becs et les cuisses sont en or : il tient dans une serre la garde d'or, et dans l'autre la lame d'acier d'un glaive antique, placé horizontalement de droite à gauche. A ce glaive est suspendue la devise Latine, en lettres d'or, " DEUS MEUMQUE JUS. " L'aigle est couronné d'un Triangle d'or : il tient une banderolle de pourpre frangée d'or et parsemée d'étoiles d'or.

ARTICLE II.

LES Insignes distinctifs des Souverains Grands Inspecteurs Généraux sont :

1o. Une Croix Teutonique rouge qui se porte sur la partie gauche de la poitrine.

2o. Un grand Cordon blanc moiré, liseré d'or ; sur le devant est un Triangle d'or radieux ; au milieu du Triangle est le chiffre 33 ; de chaque côté de l'angle supérieur du Triangle est un glaive d'argent dont la pointe se dirige vers le centre, porte de droite à gauche et se

* Blanc.

pendet latina inscriptio, " DEUS MEUMQUE JUS," aureis litteris effecta. Aquila pro coronâ aureum triangulum, tæniam habet purpuream cum aureâ fimbriâ, aureisque astris.

ARTICULUS II.

Insignia distinguentia Supremos-Magnos-Inspectores-Generales sunt :

1° Crux Teutonica rubri coloris, sinistro pectoris lateri affixa ;

2° Major funiculus albus, superficie undulatè micante, auro intextus, gerens in anteriori parte aureum triangulum aureis radiis micans, quod habet in centro notam XXXIII, atque hinc unum argenteum gladium, indè alterum, ex superioribus lateribus trianguli versùs centrum directos. Funiculus hic è dextro humero ad lævum

---

APPENDIX

TO

THE FUNDAMENTAL STATUTES AND GRAND CONSTITUTIONS OF THE SUPREME COUNCIL OF THE THIRTY-THIRD DEGREE.

ARTICLE I.

The Banner of THE ORDER is *argent*,* bordered with a fringe of gold, and having in the centre a double-headed black Eagle, its wings displayed, beaks and legs *or*, holding with one claw the hilt, *or*, and with the other the blade, *steel*, of a sword placed horizontally, hilt to the right and point to the left. From the sword hangs, lettered, *or*, the motto, in Latin, "DEUS MEUM-QUE JUS." The Eagle is crowned with a Triangle of gold, and a purple fillet, fringed and starred with gold.

ARTICLE II.

The distinctive insignia of Sovereign Grand Inspectors General are :

1. A red Teutonic Cross, worn over the left breast.

2. A broad white watered Ribbon, bordered with gold, and having on the front a golden Triangle, glittering with rays of gold, in the centre whereof is the number 33 ; and on each side of the upper angle of the Triangle is a sword of silver pointing towards

* White.

progrediens, terminatur acumine cum aureâ fimbriâ, et habente in medio tæniam coccienei sinopisque* coloris, in rotundam formam versam, tenentemque communia insignia ORDINIS.

3° Insignia hæc sunt : Aquila similis illi quæ in Vexillo est ; coronatur Aquila aureo Borussiæ Diademate.

4° Majora insignia ORDINIS affiguntur suprà Crucem Teutonicam ; suntque astrum novem habens acumina, utpotè effectum tribus aureis triangulis, unum alteri superimpositis et simul intextis. Ex inferiori parte sinistri lateris versùs superiorem dextri gladius procedit ; in oppositâ directione est manus quæ *Justitiæ* vocatur. In medio, Scutum ORDINIS, cyaneum, et in eo Aquila similis illi

* Gallicè et anglicè " Sinople," id est, Prasini coloris.

---

termine en pointe par une frange d'or et une rosette rouge et vert à laquelle est suspendu le Bijou ordinaire de l'ORDRE.

3o. Ce Bijou est un aigle semblable à celui de l'Étendard : il porte le diadème d'or de Prusse.

4o. La grande décoration de l'ORDRE est gravée sur une croix Teutonique ; c'est une étoile à neuf pointes, formée par trois triangles d'or superposés et entrelacés. Un glaive se dirige de la partie inférieure du côté gauche à la partie supérieure du côté droit, et, du côté opposé, est une main de *Justice*. Au milieu est le Bouclier de l'ORDRE, *azur ;* sur le Bouclier est un aigle semblable à celui de l'Étendard ; sur le côté droit du Bouclier est une balance d'or ; sur le côté gauche, un compas d'or posé sur une Equerre d'or. Tout autour du Bouclier est une banderolle bleue portant, en lettres d'or, l'inscription Latine " ORDO AB CHAO." Cette banderolle est enfermée dans un double cercle, formé par deux serpents d'or, chacun d'eux tenant sa queue entre les dents. Des petits triangles formés par l'intersection des triangles principaux, les neuf qui sont le plus rapprochés de la banderolle sont de couleur rouge et portent chacun une des lettres dont se compose le mot S.A.P.I.E.N.T.I.A.

5o. Les trois premiers Officiers du SUPRÊME CONSEIL portent, en outre, une écharpe ou ceinture à franges d'or et tombant du coté droit.

quæ in Vexillo est, habensque in dextro latere auream libram, et in sinistro aureum circinum, aureæ normæ intextum. Circà totum Scutum percurrit fascia cyanea cum aureâ inscriptione latinâ "ORDO AB CHAO :" quæ fascia hinc indè comprehenditur duobus circulis effectis ex duobus aureis anguibus unoquoque caudam sibi mordente. Ex miuoribus triangulis ab intersectione majorum genitis, ea novem quæ fasciæ propinquiora sunt, rubrum colorem habent, et eorum unumquodque gerit unam ex litteris quæ verbum S.A.P.I.E.N.T.I.A. efficiunt.

5° Tres primi Officiales Supremi Concilii gerunt insuper, album balteum—hoc est fasciam—auream fimbriam habentem, et à dextro latere dependentem.

---

its centre. This Ribbon, worn from the right shoulder to the left, ends in a point, with gold fringe, and has at the junction a rosette of crimson and leek-green ribbon, whereon is the general jewel of THE ORDER.

3. This jewel is an Eagle, like that on the Banner, wearing the golden diadem of Prussia.

4. The Grand Decorations of THE ORDER rest on a Teutonic Cross. They are a nine-pointed Star, formed by three Triangles of gold, one upon the other, and interlaced. From the lower part of the left side towards the upper part of the right extends a Sword, and in the opposite direction a hand of *Justice*. In the middle is the Shield of THE ORDER, *azure;* upon the Shield is an Eagle like that on the Banner ; on the dexter side of the Shield is a golden Balance, and on the sinister a golden Compass resting on a golden Square. Around the whole shield runs a stripe of azure, lettered in gold with the Latin words "ORDO AB CHAO ;" and this stripe is enclosed by a double circle, formed by two Serpents of gold, each holding his tail in his mouth. Of the smaller triangles formed by the intersection of the principal ones, those nine that are nearest the azure stripe are colored red, and on each is one of the letters that constitute the word S.A.P.I.E.N.T.I.A.

5. The first three Officers of the Supreme Council wear also a white scarf or sash, fringed with gold, hanging from the right side.

ARTICULUS III.

MAGNUM SIGILLUM ORDINIS est Scutum argenteum gerens Aquilam bicipitem similem illi quæ in Vexillo ORDINIS est, coronatam quidem aureo Borussiæ diademate, super quod est aureum triangulum radians, habens in medio notam XXXIII ; etiam potest Aquila aut coronam aut triangulum tantùm super se habere.

In inferiori Scuti parte, sub alis pedibusque Aquilæ sunt aureæ triginta tres Stellæ in semicirculum dispositæ. Totum circumdatum est inscriptione : " SUPREMUM CONCILIUM XXXIII[1] GRADUS IN . . . . . . "

ACTUM in SUPREMO CONCILIO XXXIII[1] gradûs, die, mense, annoque ut suprà.

ARTICLE III.

LE GRAND SCEAU DE L'ORDRE est un Écu d'argent sur lequel est un Aigle à deux têtes, semblable à celui de l'Étendard, mais portant de plus le diadême d'or de Prusse ; au-dessus du diadême est un Triangle radieux, au centre duquel est le chiffre 33. Toutefois, on peut se contenter de mettre au-dessus de l'Aigle, soit la couronne, soit le triangle seulement.

Au bas du Bouclier, au-dessous des ailes et des serres de l'Aigle, il y a trente-trois Etoiles disposées en demi-cercle ; tout autour est l'inscription suivante : SUPRÊME CONSEIL DU TRENTE-TROISIÈME DEGRÉ POUR . . . . . .

FAIT en SUPRÊME CONSEIL du Trente-troisième Degré, les jours, mois et an que dessus.

Signé " . . . . . . (*) . . . . . . " — " STARK. " — " d'ESTERNO." — " . . . . . . (*) . . . . . . " — " H. WILLHELM. " — " D . . . . . . " — " WŒLLNER."

APPROUVÉ,
  L. S.   *Signé,*   FRÉDÉRIC.

NOTE.

(*) Ces *astérisques* (aux *pages* 136 et 144) désignent les places de quelques signatures devenues illisibles, ou qui sont effacées par l'effet du frottement, ou par l'eau de la mer, à laquelle l'ampliation originale de ces documents, écrits sur parchemin, a été accidentellement exposée plusieurs fois.

(Subscriptum) "......(*)......" — " STARK."— " D'ESTERNO."
— " ....(*)......." " — "H. WILLELM." — "D......."
" WOELLNER."

APPROBATUM.

L. S.   Subscriptum,   "FREDERICUS."

ARTICLE III.

THE GREAT SEAL of THE ORDER is a silver Shield, bearing a double-headed Eagle, like that upon the Banner of THE ORDER, but crowned with the golden diadem of Prussia, and over that a Triangle of gold, emitting rays, and in its centre the number 33. The Eagle may, however, be surmounted by either the crown or triangle alone.

At the base of the Shield, under the wings and claws of the Eagle, are 33 golden stars in a semicircle. Around the whole is this inscription: "SUPREME COUNCIL OF THE 33D DEGREE FOR....."

DONE in SUPREME COUNCIL of the 33d degree, the day, month and year above mentioned.

(Signed) " ......(*)......" "STARK." — "D'ESTERNO." —
" ....(*)........." — "H. WILLELM." — "D........." —
"WŒLLNER."

APPROVED.

(L. S.)   *Signed,*   "FREDERIC."

NOTE.

(*) The *asterisks* (at *pages* 137 and 145 English, and pages 136 and 145 Latin,) mark the places of certain signatures that have become illegible or been effaced by attrition, or by the effect of sea-water, to which the original duplicate of these documents, written on parchment, has several times been accidentally exposed.

REGULATIONS AND RESOLUTIONS

OF

THE SUPREME GRAND COUNCIL

OF

SOV.˙. GR.˙. INSPECTORS GENERAL

FOR

THE NORTHERN JURISDICTION OF THE UNITED STATES.

DECREES ENACTED IN 1851.

Decreed, That each Grand Council of Princes of Jerusalem and each Consistory of S. P. R. S., within this jurisdiction, be allowed to send *three* delegates to meet in council of deliberation, with this S. G. C., when open in its Sovereign G. Council of Princes of Jerusalem, and Sovereign Grand Consistory S. P. R. S., at its annual and other Grand Convocations.

Decreed, That all "District Deputies," as well as all "Special Deputies" of this S. G. C., be furnished with patents, particularly defining the powers to be exercised by them.

Decreed, That this S. G. C. cause strictly to be enforced the salutary constitutional regulations that the 30th, 31st and 32d degrees, shall under no circumstances whatever, be conferred by any private Consistory, unless by special dispensation from the Sov. G. Commander of the Sup. G. Council first had and obtained.

Decreed, That no diplomas or certificates shall be valid unless emanating from this Supreme Grand Council.

Decreed, That every application for warrants or charters, diplomas or certificates, be required in the first instance to be made to the Deputy of the District in which the applicant resides; and it shall be the duty of the Deputy applied to, to make immediate report of such application to the Ill. G. Secretary General.

All such applications from Districts for which there are no Deputies appointed, and all other communications regarding "the Ineffable and Sublime Degrees," must be made directly to *Charles W. Moore, Ill. G. Secretary General, Boston, Mass.*

In 1852.

Decreed, That all Bodies holding under the authority and owing allegiance to this Supreme Council, are required to make their returns directly to the Ill. Secretary General of this Supreme Council, at Boston.

Decreed, That each and every organization working under the authority of this Supreme Council, be, and it hereby is, allowed a representation by its first three officers, in the "Councils of Deliberation," holden by this Supreme Council, at its Annual and other Grand Convocations, when open in the appropriate degree; said representatives not being of a lower grade than that of Princes of Jerusalem.

In 1853.

Resolved, That the Supreme Council recognize the principle that a Charter shall not issue to any body that has not been regularly organized, and worked under Dispensation at least six months.

In 1857.

Ordered, That the minimum rate of fees for the Bodies under this jurisdiction shall be as follows, viz:—

Degrees in the Grand Lodges of Perfection,	$20 00
Fee to Supreme Council for each Candidate,	1 00
Degrees in Chapters of Princes of Jerusalem,	10 00
Fee for each one created Prince,	1 00
Degrees in Chapter of Rose-Croix,	15 00
Fee of each Prince exalted, - -	1 00
Degrees in the Consistory, - - -	50 00
Register and Initiation fees, each Companion exalted,	2 00
If the Consistory confers the degrees of Rose-Croix and its own, the fees shall be, - - - -	3 00

Grand Lodge of Perfection, - - - - - - 25 00
Chapter of Princes of Jerusalem, - 25 00
Chapter of Rose-Croix, - - - 25 00
Consistory, 32d, - -, - - 50 00
Charter for Consistory, with power to confer Rose-Croix De-
grees, - - 60 00
Charter for Consistory, covering all minor Bodies, 100 00

ANNUAL DUES TO THE SUPREME COUNCIL FROM THE SEVERAL BODIES.

Grand Lodge of Perfection, - $5 00
Chapter of Princes of Jerusalem, - 3 00
Chapter of Rose-Croix, - - - 3 00
Consistory, 32d, - - 5 00
If the above Bodies are included in a Charter of Consistory,
the fees for all shall be - 10 00
Fees to the Grand Secretary Gen. of the H. E. for each
Charter issued, in addition to the amount to Supreme
Council, - 10 00

All of which shall be paid before the Dispensation or Charter is
issued.

Resolved, That every candidate for the degrees in this Consistory, residing within one hundred miles of the Grand East of the
Northern Jurisdiction, shall make known his desire, one month, at
least, before the annual meeting of this Council, and if approved
by.the Grand Commander and Secretary General, his application
for the degrees may be made, and not otherwise.

In 1858.

Resolved, That the G. Sec. Gen. be and is hereby requested to
report to this Council the name and location of each Body subordinate to this Sup. Grand Council.

Resolved, That the Grand Treasurer Gen. be and is hereby requested to report to this Council the date of the last Return made
from each Subordinate Body.

Resolved, That the G. Sec. General be instructed to procure
printed copies of the Record of the Sup. Council, interleaved and
bound similar to the volume present, sufficient to present one to

each of the Sov. Grand Inspectors that are recognized and privileged to act in this Council.

Ordered, That the minimum rate of fees for conferring the Degrees by the bodies under this jurisdiction shall be as follows, viz.:

Degrees in the Lodge of Perfection, -	$30 00
Degrees in Council of Princes of Jerusalem,	20 00
Degrees in Chapter of Rose-Croix, -	25 00
Degrees in Consistory,	50 00
Total,	$125 00

Resolved, That the subject of *Certificates* be referred to the Supreme Council, with recommendation that it furnish the Bodies subordinate thereto with such Certificates, and enjoin upon them the use thereof, in case of each member now or hereafter to be created, and that Masonic intercourse be interdicted with those residing within this jurisdiction who do not possess them; and further, that the Supreme Council be requested to bring this subject favorably to the notice of the several Supreme Grand Councils with which it is in correspondence, to the end that, if adopted by them, the system may become universal, and add greatly to the peace and security of all regular and legitimate Supreme Councils throughout the world.

11

SUPREME COUNCIL

FOR

THE SOUTHERN JURISDICTION OF THE UNITED STATES.

ESTABLISHED AS THE ONLY SUPREME COUNCIL FOR THE UNITED STATES, 31ST MAY, 1801, AT CHARLESTON.

JOHN MITCHELL; M∴ P∴ Sov∴ Gr∴ Commander,	. 1801
FREDERICK DALCHO; Lt∴ Gr∴ Commander,	. . 1801
EMANUEL DE LA MOTTA; Treasurer Gen∴ H∴ E∴,	. 1802
ABRAHAM ALEXANDER; Secretary Gen∴ H∴ E∴,	. 1802
THOMAS B. BOWEN; Gr∴ Master of Ceremonies,	. 1802
ISRAEL DE LIEBEN; Sov∴ Gr∴ Insp∴ Gen∴,	. . 1802
ISAAC AULD; Sov∴ Gr∴ Insp∴ Gen∴,	. . . 1802
MOSES C. LEVY; Sov∴ Gr∴ Insp∴ Gen∴, .	. . 1802
JAMES MOULTRIE; Sov∴ Gr∴ Insp∴ Gen∴, .	. . 1802

SUPREME COUNCIL IN 1813.

John Mitchell, admitted in	1801
Frederick Dalcho, M. D., ...	1801
Emanuel de la Motta, ...	1802
Isaac Auld, ...	1802
James Moultrie, ...	1802

SUPREME COUNCIL IN 1825.

Frederick Dalcho, admitted	1801
James Moultrie,	1802
Emanuel de la Motta,	1802
Moses Holbrook,	1822
Horatio G. Street,	1822
Alexander McDonald,	1822
Jos. McCosh,	1822
Jacob de la Motta,	1823

SUPREME COUNCIL IN 1844.

Alexander McDonald,	1822
Horatio G. Street,	1822
Jos. McCosh,	1822
Jacob de la Motta,	1823
John Roche,	1825
Joseph Eveleth,	1825
Cornelius C. Sebring,	1826
Albert G. Mackey,	1844
Albert Case,	1844

SUPREME COUNCIL IN 1846.

Alexander McDonald, admitted in	1822
Horatio G. Street, "	1822
Jos. McCosh,	1822
C. C. Sebring, (removed and vacated),	1826
Albert G. Mackey,	1844
Albert Case,	1844
John H. Honour,	1845
James C. Norris,	1845
James S. Burges,	1845
Charles M. Furman,	1845

SUPREME COUNCIL IN 1855.

Joseph McCosh, ... 1822
Albert G. Mackey, ... 1844
John H. Honour, ... 1845
Charles M. Furman, ... 1845
William S. Rockwell, ... 1847
John R. McDaniel, ... 1847
John A. Quitman, ... 1848
Achille Le Prince, ... · 1850

MEMBERS ON THE 1st OF MARCH, 1859.

ALBERT PIKE, of Little Rock, Arkansas, Most Puissant Sov∴
Gr∴ Commander : admitted in 1858

CHARLES M. FURMAN, of Charleston, So∴ Car∴ Puissant
Lieutenant Grand Commander : admitted in . . 1845

ACHILLE LE PRINCE, of Charleston, So∴ Car∴ Ill∴ Treasurer
General of the H∴ E∴: admitted in 1850

ALBERT G. MACKEY, of Charleston, So∴ Car∴ Ill∴ Secretary
General of the H∴ E∴: admitted in 1844

JOHN H. HONOUR, of Charleston, So∴ Car∴ Sov∴ Gr∴ Insp∴
Gen∴ : admitted in 1845

WILLIAM S. ROCKWELL, of Savannah, Georgia, Sov∴ Gr∴
Insp∴ Gen∴: admitted in 1847

JOHN ROBIN McDANIEL, of Lynchburg, Va∴ Sov∴ Gr∴ Insp∴
Gen∴ : admitted in 1847

CLAUDE SAMORY, of New Orleans, Louisiana, Sov∴ Gr∴ Insp∴
Gen∴ : admitted in 1856

CHARLES LAFFON DE LADEBAT, of New Orleans, La∴ Sov∴
Gr∴ Insp∴ Gen∴ : admitted in 1859

ADDITIONAL MEMBERS UP TO OCTOBER 1st, 1859.

10. Benj. Rush Campbell, of Laurensville, So.˙. Car.˙., Sov.˙. Gr.˙. Insp.˙. Gen.˙.

11. Hugh Parks Watson, of Montgomery, Alabama, Sov.˙. Gr.˙. Insp.˙. Gen.˙.

12. Giles M. Hillyer, of Natchez, Mississippi, Sov.˙. Gr.˙. Insp.˙. Gen.˙.

13. John R. Batchelor, of New Orleans, Louisiana, Sov.˙. Gr.˙. Insp.˙. Gen.˙.

14. Charles Scott, of Memphis, Tennessee, Sov.˙. Gr.˙. Insp.˙. Gen.˙.

15. James Penn, of Memphis, Tennessee, Sov.˙. Gr.˙. Insp.˙. Gen.˙.

16. Frederick Webber, of Louisville, Kentucky, Sov.˙. Gr.˙. Insp.˙. Gen.˙.

17. Luke E. Barber, of Little Rock, Arkansas, Sov.˙. Gr.˙. Insp.˙. Gen.˙.

18. Anthony O'Sullivan, of St. Louis, Missouri, Sov.˙. Gr.˙. Insp.˙. Gen.˙.

19. Theodore S. Parvin, of Muscatine, Iowa, Sov.˙. Gr.˙. Insp.˙. Gen.˙.

20. Azariah T. C. Pierson, of St. Paul, Minnesota, Sov.˙. Gr.˙. Insp.˙. Gen.˙.

ELECTED, BUT NOT YET ADMITTED.

21. Benjamin B. French, District of Columbia.
22. E. H. Gill, Richmond, Virginia.
23. Thomas Brown, Tallahassee, Florida.
24. Edward R. Ives, Lake City, Florida.
25. J. McCaleb Wiley, Troy, Alabama.
26. William P. Mellen, Natchez, Mississippi.
27. John C. Breckenridge, Lexington, Kentucky.

VACANCIES TO BE FILLED.

28. Texas, one.
29. Maryland, one.
30. North Carolina, one.
31. Georgia, one.
32. Missouri, one.
33. California, one.

SUPREME GRAND COUNCIL

FOR

THE NORTHERN JURISDICTION OF THE UNITED STATES.

ESTABLISHED JAN. 7, 1815, AT NEW YORK, AND SINCE REMOVED TO BOSTON

ORIGINAL MEMBERS.

DANIEL D. TOMPKINS; M∴ P∴ Sov∴ Gr∴ Commander;
SAMPSON SIMSON; Lieut∴ Gr∴ Commander;
JOHN GABRIEL TARDY;
JOHN JAMES JOSEPH GOURGAS;
MOSES LEVY MADURO PEIXOTTO;
RICHARD RIKER.

PRESENT MEMBERS: 1859.

EDWARD A. RAYMOND, of Boston, Sov∴ Gr∴ Commander. *Ad vitam.*

ROBERT P. DUNLAP,* of Brunswick, Me∴ M∴ Ill∴ Lieut. G∴ Commander.

SIMON W. ROBINSON, of Lexington, Mass∴ Ill∴ G∴ Treasurer General H∴ E∴

CHARLES W. MOORE, of Boston, Ill∴ Gr∴ Sec∴ Gen∴ H∴ E∴

REV. ALBERT CASE, of Boston, Assist∴ Gr∴ Sec∴ Gen∴ H∴ E∴

AMMI B. YOUNG, of Washington, D. C., Ill∴ G∴ Capt. L∴ G∴

WILLIAM B. HUBBARD, of Columbus, Ohio, Sov∴ G∴ Insp∴ Gen∴ H∴ E∴

CHARLES GILMAN, of Baltimore, Sov∴ Gr∴ Insp∴ General.

C. R. STARKWEATHER, of Chicago, Illinois, Sov∴ Gr∴ Insp∴ General.

DISTRICT DEPUTIES.

GILES F. YATES, of New York, Deputy for New York.

JOHN CHRISTIE, of Portsmouth, N. H., Sov∴ Gr∴ Insp∴ Gen∴ 33°, Deputy for New Hampshire.

KILLAN H. VAN RENSSELAER, of Cambridge, Ohio, Sov∴ Gr∴ Insp∴ Gen∴ 33°. Deputy for Western Penn. and Ohio.

Died October 20, 1859.

Constitutions of 1859.

CONSTITUTIONS OF 1859.

𝔇eus meumque 𝔍us.

THE Sovereign Grand Inspectors General of the 33d and Last degree of the Ancient and Accepted Scottish Rite for the Southern Jurisdiction of the United States, duly assembled in Supreme Council of the 33d degree, at the Council Chamber in Charleston, on the 19th day of the Hebrew month ואדר, A∴ M∴ 5619, which answers to the 25th day of March, A∴D∴ 1859, in pursuance of the Order of the M∴ P∴ Sov∴ Grand Commander, and after due notification given to all the Sov∴ Gr∴ Inspectors General, in writing, do, upon full consideration and deliberation, adopt and enact the following

GENERAL STATUTES AND REGULATIONS

OF THE

SUPREME COUNCIL FOR THE SOUTHERN JURISDICTION OF THE UNITED STATES

ARTICLE I.

THE number of active members of the Supreme Council is hereby increased and enlarged to, and forever fixed at, thirty-three, including therein the nine existing members. The jurisdiction of this Supreme Council includes all the United States and the Territories thereof, except the States of Maine, Massachusetts, Vermont, New Hampshire, Rhode Island, Connecticut, New York, New Jersey, Pennsylvania, Ohio, Indiana, Illinois, Michigan and Wisconsin, which were apportioned to the Supreme Council for the Northern Jurisdiction of the United States, at its creation in the year 1815, and the State of Delaware, which, upon the application of that Council in the year 1827, this Council permitted to be included in the Northern Jurisdiction.

ARTICLE II.

The said thirty-three members shall be apportioned as follows :

To the State of Maryland,	One.
To the District of Columbia,	One.
To the State of Virginia,	Two.
To the State of North Carolina,	One.
To the State of South Carolina,	Five.
To the State of Georgia,	Two.
To the State of Florida,	Two.
To the State of Alabama,	Two.
To the State of Mississippi,	Two.
To the State of Louisiana,	Three.
To the State of Tennessee,	Two.
To the State of Kentucky,	Two.
To the State of Texas,	One.
To the State of Arkansas,	Two.
To the State of Missouri,	Two.
To the State of Iowa,	One.
To the State of Minnesota,	One.
To the State of California,	One.

ARTICLE III.

Whenever vacancies shall occur hereafter, by death, resignation, or other cause, of members from States other than South Carolina, having more than one member, they shall be filled by members, first from Oregon, next from Kansas, and then from any other new States in the Jurisdiction, until each State shall have at least one member; after which each vacancy shall be filled by a member from the same State as the person whose place is to be filled: but the State of South Carolina shall always have five members.

ARTICLE IV.

Whenever a vacancy is to be filled by election of a person from a State in which a Grand Consistory shall have been established and be in activity. such Grand Consistory shall be notified thereof by the Secretary General, and shall thereupon nominate three persons having at least the rank of Sublime Prince of the Royal Secret, to the Supreme Council, as candidates for the vacancy ; one of whom the Supreme Council shall elect to fill the same ; the unanimous vote of all the members present being necessary to a choice.

For States wherein there is no Grand Consistory, the Supreme Council shall elect without previous nomination.

ARTICLE V.

All such elections must be held by the Supreme Council when in session, and the vote be taken *viva voce*. And no person can be elected a member of the Supreme Council unless he has attained the 32d degree, and is at least thirty-five years of age.

ARTICLE VI.

The officers of the Supreme Council shall be :

1st. The Most Puissant Sovereign Grand Commander;
2d. The Puissant Sovereign Lieutenant Grand Commander ;
3d. The Ill.·. Secretary-General of the Holy Empire, who shall be the Keeper of the Seals and Archives ;
4th. The Ill.·. Treasurer-General of the Holy Empire ;
5th. The Ill.·. Grand Minister of State ;
6th. The Ill.·. Grand Hospitaller ;
7th. The Ill.·. Grand Marshal ;
8th. The Ill.·. Grand Standard-Bearer ;
9th. The Ill.·. Grand Captain of the Guards ;
10th. The Ill.·. Gr.·. Master of Ceremonies.

And there shall also be an Ill.·. Grand Tiler, who must possess the 33d Degree of Deputy Grand Inspector General.

ARTICLE VII.

When a vacancy occurs in the office of Sov.·. Grand Commander, Lt.·. Gr.·. Commander, Secretary General, or Treasurer General, it shall be filled by election, a majority of the votes of all the members of the Council being necessary to a choice. Vacancies in the other offices shall be filled by appointment by the M.·. P.·. Sov.·. Grand Commander.

ARTICLE VIII.

All the officers are elected or appointed for life, and the members are also for life: Provided, That Office or Membership shall be forfeited, *ipso facto*, by permanent removal of the party beyond the jurisdiction.

ARTICLE IX.

No Sov.·. Gr.·. Inspector General can hereafter vote in the Supreme Council by proxy, when personally absent.

ARTICLE X.

The Supreme Council shall meet annually, at the Grand Orient of Charleston, South Carolina, on the second Monday of January, at 7 o'clock, P. M.; and special meetings may be called by the Sov.·. Gr.·. Commander at any time, to be held at the same place.

ARTICLE XI.

Seven Sovereign Grand Inspectors General, the Sov.·. Gr.·. Commander or Lt.·. Gr.·. Commander being one, shall constitute a quorum for the transaction of business.

ARTICLE XII.

An active member, who by reason of age or infirmity, shall resign his seat, will become an *Emeritus* Member. The Supreme Council may elect as Honorary Members, such Sovereign Grand Inspectors General as may have removed or may remove from another jurisdiction into this; or such Deputy Grand Inspectors General as may be created within this jurisdiction, by authority of the Supreme Council.

ARTICLE XIII.

Emeritus and Honorary Members are entitled to sit in the Supreme Council at all times, except during an election of a member to supply a vacancy therein.

ARTICLE XIV.

In all cases of election to Honorary Membership, the vote must be unanimous, one negative vote being sufficient to refuse that mark of honor and confidence.

ARTICLE XV.

Whenever any vote whatever is needed to be taken in the recess of the Supreme Council, the Secretary General will by letter state the question to each Sov.·. Grand Inspector General, who will in writing and by letter transmit to him his vote; and when all are received, or after sufficient time has elapsed for all to respond, the Secretary General will declare the result.

ARTICLE XVI.

In all cases where any Sov.·. Grand Inspector General, being so called on, fails in a reasonable time to transmit his vote, he will be deemed to have assented to the action of the majority required in

the given case; and whenever one duly notified fails to attend a called session, or, without notification, to attend a regular session, he will be deemed to have assented to the action of the majority present, in all cases; and is to be forever afterwards estopped to deny that he assented thereto.

ARTICLE XVII.

A Sovereign Grand Inspector General, habitually absenting himself from the meetings of the Supreme Council, may be declared, by vote of two-thirds of all the members, taken by yeas and nays, to have virtually resigned his membership; and thereupon the vacancy so occurring may be filled in the usual manner.

ARTICLE XVIII.

At every annual meeting of the Supreme Council, it shall hold also a Consistory of the 32d degree, composed of the members of the Supreme Council, and of two delegates from each Consistory of Sublime Princes of the Royal Secret, 32d degree, under its jurisdiction. In this Consistorial Chamber shall be heard and considered all appeals from and questions referred by the Consistories, and all complaints from Subordinate Bodies: and such Chamber may also suggest and recommend measures for the consideration of the Supreme Council. From its decisions an appeal will in all cases lie to the Supreme Council.

ARTICLE XIX.

The Supreme Council reserves to itself the power of conferring any of the degrees of the Ancient and Accepted Scottish Rite, upon such persons as it may deem worthy to receive them. It may delegate that power to Deputy Grand Inspectors General, to be exercised in foreign countries wherein no Supreme Council has been established; and in States of the United States wherein there is no Consistory of Sublime Princes of the Royal Secret: but no such Deputy Grand Inspector General can confer the 33d Degree.

ARTICLE XX.

Each member of the Supreme Council is also, by virtue of his office, authorized to confer any of the degrees except the 33d, in any Foreign Country where no Supreme Council is established, and in any State of the United States, where there is no Consistory of Sublime Princes of the Royal Secret.

ARTICLE XXI.

The 33d Degree, of Deputy Grand Inspector General, may be conferred by the Supreme Council, upon any person duly and unanimously elected to receive it ; or by a single Sovereign Grand Inspector General, active member of the Supreme Council, by special authorization and order of the Supreme Council, on any person so elected, when such person resides elsewhere than in the State of South Carolina.

ARTICLE XXII.

The Revenues of the Supreme Council shall be derived from the charge for Charters, from that for Letters-Patent of the 32d Degree, and from a tax on all Bodies under its jurisdiction, and for all degrees conferred by Sovereign or Deputy Grand Inspectors General.

ARTICLE XXIII.

The charge for every Charter for a Consistory of the 32d Degree shall be fifty dollars; for an Areopagus of Knights Kadosh, forty dollars ; for a Chapter of Rose-Croix, thirty dollars ; for a Council of Princes of Jerusalem, twenty-five dollars; for a Lodge of Perfection, twenty dollars; and for a Council of Royal and Select Masters, twenty dollars.

ARTICLE XXIV.

All Letters-Patent or of Credence of the 32d Degree shall emanate from the Supreme Council, and shall not be granted by the Consistories ; but if one is desired by a Prince of the Royal Secret, his Consistory shall give him a certificate of possession of the 32d Degree, signed by the Commander in Chief, and countersigned by its Chancellor, under its seal; upon presentation whereof to the Secretary General, the Letters-Patent and of Credence shall issue.

ARTICLE XXV.

The charge for Letters-Patent and of Credence of the 32d Degree shall be five dollars, and the fee of the Secretary General, one dollar in addition. The fee for Letters-Patent of the 33d Degree, of Deputy or Sovereign Grand Inspector General, shall be ten dollars, out of which shall be retained by or paid to the Secretary General, his fee of two dollars and fifty cents.

ARTICLE XXVI.

The fees for the several degrees, when conferred by the Supreme Council, or by a Sovereign or Deputy Grand Inspector General, shall be as follows:

For the degrees from the 4th to the 14th inclusive, $10
For the 15th and 16th, ... 5
For the 17th and 18th, ... 15
From the 19th to the 30th inclusive, . . . 15
For the 31st and 32d, ... 15
For the degrees of Royal and Select Master, . 10

ARTICLE XXVII.

All Charters shall be prepared and sealed by the Secretary General, who shall receive as his fee for each, in addition to the charge above fixed for such Charter, the sum of fifteen dollars.

ARTICLE XXVIII.

All fees received from Sovereign or Deputy Grand Inspectors General, for degrees conferred by them, shall be accounted for by them, and paid over to the Supreme Council, deducting therefrom only their travelling expenses necessarily incurred in the service of the Order, the accounts whereof shall be audited and approved by the Supreme Council.

ARTICLE XXIX.

No Consistory, Council, Chapter, or Lodge of Perfection, shall confer any of the degrees for any less fees than those hereinbefore, in Section xxvi., provided; but it is allowed to either or any of such bodies to increase the amounts at their pleasure.

ARTICLE XXX.

Each body under the jurisdiction of this Supreme Council shall annually, on the first day of December, remit to the Supreme Council the following tax, for and on account of its members, and of the degrees conferred by it, not theretofore accounted for; that is to say:

Each Consistory of Sublime Princes of the Royal Secret, one dollar for each person then a member of it; and for each case in which the 32d degree had been conferred during the year in and by such body, three dollars.

Each Council of Knights Kadosch, Chapter of Rose-Croix, and Council of Princes of Jerusalem, one dollar for each person then a member of it; and for each case in which, during the year, the highest degree given in each such body respectively has been conferred, two dollars.

Each Lodge of Perfection and Council of Royal and Select Masters, fifty cents for each person then a member of it ; and for each case in which, during the year, the highest degree given in each such body respectively has been conferred, one dollar.

ARTICLE XXXI.

In each State where a Consistory of Sublime Princes of the Royal Secret is in existence and working, the fees and tax of the subordinate bodies shall be paid to such Consistory, which shall pay to the Supreme Council only the tax for its own members of one dollar each per annum, and the fee of three dollars for each person on whom it confers the 32d degree.

ARTICLE XXXII.

The Supreme Council shall have jurisdiction over the Councils of Royal and Select Masters in every State where no Grand Council of those degrees has been established ; and such Councils shall make their returns and pay their tax to the Supreme Council; but so soon as there are three such Councils in any such State, the Supreme Council shall recommend to such Councils to establish a Grand Council, and upon the establishment of the same the jurisdiction of the Supreme Council over such Councils shall cease.

ARTICLE XXXIII.

Every Sov∴ Grand Inspector General of this jurisdiction will be, by virtue of his office, a member of each Grand Council of Royal and Select Masters so created, if he has legally received these degrees, and these bodies will in all cases be created on that express condition.

ARTICLE XXXIV.

Only one Consistory shall be established in each State within this jurisdiction ; and the title of each shall be: "The M∴ Puissant Sovereign Grand Consistory of Sublime Princes of the Royal Secret, 32d Degree of the Ancient and Accepted Scottish Rite, in and for the State of A. . . . ."

ARTICLE XXXV.

Each such Grand Consistory shall consist of not less than nine members. It shall be the Deputy of this Supreme Council, and the governing power of the Ancient and Accepted Rite in the State wherein it is organized; and from it, after its organization and installation, all charters for bodies of the Degrees below the 31st, in such State, shall emanate; and all Patents, Briefs and Diplomas for the degrees from the 14th to the 30th, inclusive ; the fees for all which shall be fixed by itself. And, until a Grand Council is established, it may also grant charters for Councils of Royal and Select Masters, and Briefs of those Degrees.

ARTICLE XXXVI.

The Secretary General will, on application, and without charge, *visé* any Diploma, Brief, or Patent, issued by a Consistory, and affix the seal of the Supreme Council to his *visa*, without charge.

ARTICLE XXXVII.

All Diplomas, Briefs and Patents, of the 14th, 16th, 30th, and 32d Degrees, will be on parchment, and in the three languages, Latin, French and English, that they may avail the holder everywhere ; and in every case he will sign his name in the margin.

ARTICLE XXXVIII.

It is recommended to each Consistory to hold, at each regular meeting, a Council of Kadosch, a Chapter of Rose-Croix, and a Sublime Grand Lodge of Perfection in its bosom, allowing to be represented in each, respectively, all the Councils, Chapters and Lodges under its jurisdiction, by proper delegates, under such regulations as it may prescribe.

ARTICLE XXXIX.

Each Consistory within this jurisdiction is at liberty, and is advised, to inaugurate and maintain a system of Correspondence and Representation with each other Consistory of this jurisdiction, but will correspond with Consistories of other and foreign jurisdictions only through this Supreme Council, through which it will transmit all communications for such foreign bodies, including those of the Northern jurisdiction of the United States.

12

ARTICLE XL.

It is absolutely forbidden hereafter to print the ritual of any of the degrees of the Ancient and Accepted Scottish Rite. It is also absolutely forbidden to issue or deliver any MS. ritual of any degree to any individual Brother, other than a Sovereign Grand Inspector General or Deputy Grand Inspector General, commissioned to confer the degrees and constitute bodies. All MS. Rituals delivered by the Supreme Council, or a Grand Consistory, shall be authenticated by its seal; as, also, shall any printed Ritual that may be, in part or in whole, adopted by the Supreme Council.

ARTICLE XLI.

No copy of the Ritual of the 33d Degree, prepared by the M∴ P∴ Sov∴ Grand Commander, and which is hereby adopted, shall ever be furnished to any one except an active member of this Supreme Council.

ARTICLE XLII.

Every Consistory must meet at least once in every six months. Every Lodge of Perfection and Council of Royal and Select Masters, once in every three months; and the other bodies, on the days prescribed in their respective rituals.

ARTICLE XLIII.

A Consistory of Sublime Princes of the Royal Secret, in any State, may request its subordinates to confer the degrees from the 4th to the 30th, inclusive, on any eminent and distinguished Mason of its own or another jurisdiction where there is no Consistory, as an *honorarium*, without fee, if, in its opinion, it will be for the benefit of the Order. It will, however, be at the option of such bodies to do so or not to do so, as they may think fit. And when these degrees have so been conferred, the same Consistory may also confer on such person the 31st and 32d Degrees as an honorarium, without fee; but, in all such cases, the vote in the Consistory and each inferior body must be unanimous. In every such case, no tax shall be paid, for the degree so conferred, by the subordinate bodies to the Consistory, or by the Consistory to the Supreme Council.

ARTICLE XLIV.

A Sovereign Grand Inspector General, active member of the Supreme Council, may also, in a State or country where there is no Consistory of Princes of the Royal Secret, in like manner confer the degrees, up to and including the 32d, on eminent and distinguished Masons, by way of honorarium, and without fee; being careful to do so only in cases where it is deserved by the highest merit, and exemplary services rendered to Masonry, and each such Sov∴ Gr∴ Insp∴ General being responsible to the Supreme Council for the proper and discreet exercise of this High Power, and being liable to censure and even destitution of office, if it be abused.

ARTICLE XLV.

It is permissible for Councils of Kadosch and Chapters of Rose-Croix to have in their bosoms bodies of the inferior degrees, or to be divided into chambers of different degrees, if they desire.

ARTICLE XLVI.

The following degrees must always hereafter be conferred, wherever the proper bodies exist with power to confer them ; and can never, under any circumstances, be communicated by such bodies, but only by Sovereign or Deputy Grand Inspectors General, in places where no such bodies have been established ; that is to say :

The Ninth, Fourteenth, Eighteenth, Thirtieth, Thirty-First and Thirty-Second.   The others may be communicated; but it is recommended to all bodies administering them, that they at intervals confer them all upon different candidates, part upon one and part upon another ; that all, receiving them in full, or seeing them conferred, may become familiar therewith.

ARTICLE XLVII.

All elections and installations of officers must take place at the meeting on, or immediately before, the festival of St. John the Evangelist ; unless by dispensation from some Sovereign Grand Inspector General, or unless otherwise directed in the ritual.

ARTICLE XLVIII.

All returns of Consistories and subordinate bodies must be made on the 1st day of December in each year, and be directed

to the Secretary General at Charleston, S. C. They must contain the names of the officers and members of the body ; and a statement of what degrees have been conferred, and the names of the persons upon whom they have been conferred, since the last return.

ARTICLE XLIX.

A Deputy Grand Inspector General, visiting an inferior body, is to be received with seven stars and seven swords, and to enter under the Arch of Steel, swords clashing and gavels beating ; a Sovereign Grand Inspector General with nine stars and nine swords ; and the M∴ P∴ Sovereign Grand Commander with eleven stars and eleven swords ; to pass under the Arch of Steel, and each with swords clashing and gavels beating. And whenever the presiding officer is not of equal rank with the visitor, he surrenders to him the Mallet of Command.

ARTICLE L.

Every Sov∴ Grand Inspector General, active member of the Supreme Council, possesses, and may exercise in the State in which he resides, during the recess of the Supreme Council, all the prerogatives of a Grand Master, so far as relates to the Ancient and Accepted Rite.

ARTICLE LI.

All the existing Statutes and Regulations of this Supreme Council are to be taken and held as superseded by these present Revised Regulations, which, with the Regulations of 1762, and the Grand Constitutions of 1786, so far as the same are unaltered hereby, and with the unwritten principles and landmarks of Freemasonry, shall henceforth be the law of the Ancient and Accepted Scottish Rite in the Southern Jurisdiction of the United States.

New Orleans Scottish Rite College
http://www.youtube.com/c/NewOrleansScottishRiteCollege

Clear, Easy to Watch
Scottish Rite and Craft Lodge
Video Education

**More Books in the Cornerstone
Scottish Rite Education Series**

**Officers of Constitution and Inauguration
of a Council of Knights Kadosh**
by Albert Pike
6x9 Softcover 110 pages
ISBN: 1613421095

Bibliography of the Writings of Albert Pike
by William L. Boyden
6x9 Softcover 88 pages
ISBN 1-453875-51-4

The Bonseigneur Rituals
Edited by Gerry L. Prinsen
Foreword by Michael R. Poll
8x10 Softcover 2 volumes 574 pages
ISBN 1-934935-34-4

Chapter Rose Croix
by Albert Pike
Foreword by Albert Mackey
6x9 Softcover 108 pages
ISBN 1-453762-02-7

The Life Story Of Albert Pike
by Fred W. Allsopp
6x9 Softcover 156 pages
ISBN 1-453756-87-6

The Grand Orient of Louisiana
*A Short History and Catechism of a
Lost French Rite Masonic Body*
Introduction by Michael R. Poll
Softcover 52 pages
ISBN 1-934935-23-9

Cornerstone Book Publishers
www.cornerstonepublishers.com